Heroism, Celebrity and Therapy in *Nurse Jackie*

This book presents an examination of the television series *Nurse Jackie*, making connections between the representational processes and the audience consumption of the series. A key point of reference is the political and performative potential of *Nurse Jackie* with regards to its progressive representation of prescription drug addiction and its relationship to the concept of quality television. It deconstructs *Nurse Jackie*'s discursive potential, involving intersections with contemporary notions of genre, heroism, celebrity, therapy and feminism. At the same time this book foregrounds the self-reflexive educational potential of the series, largely enabled by the scriptwriters and the leading actor Edie Falco.

Christopher Pullen is a principal academic in Media Theory at Bournemouth University, Dorset, in the United Kingdom. He has published widely on sexuality and the media, with a particular focus on LGBT identity. His recent work includes a focus on HIV/AIDS narratives and the significance of personal autobiography, and his forthcoming work focuses on queer youth refugees in media documentary.

Routledge Focus on Television Studies

The Evolution of Black Women in Television
Mammies, Matriarchs and Mistresses
Imani M. Cheers

Heroism, Celebrity and Therapy in *Nurse Jackie*
Christopher Pullen

For more information about this series, please visit: www.routledge.com

Heroism, Celebrity and Therapy in *Nurse Jackie*

Christopher Pullen

Routledge
Taylor & Francis Group

LONDON AND NEW YORK

First published 2019
by Routledge

2 Park Square, Milton Park, Abingdon, Oxfordshire OX14 4RN
52 Vanderbilt Avenue, New York, NY 10017

Routledge is an imprint of the Taylor & Francis Group, an informa business

First issued in paperback 2020

Library of Congress Cataloging-in-Publication Data
A catalog record for this book has been requested

ISBN: 978-1-138-23850-3 (hbk)
ISBN: 978-0-367-60688-6 (pbk)

Typeset in Times New Roman
by Apex CoVantage, LLC

For Edie Falco

Contents

Figures

Preface

Edie Falco, the lead character in the landmark television drama series *Nurse Jackie* (2009–15), tells us in interview:

> Some of my biggest emotions that I felt in my life were actually in the guise of a different person, but they store themselves in my body so I feel like I experienced that, and I did.
>
> (AAT 2018)

Falco's ability to blur the real life with the experiential offers a central premise of engagement in our understanding of *Nurse Jackie*. The television series was revolutionary for its representation of prescription drug addiction, largely made vivid through Falco openly discussing her own history of (alcohol) addiction within public interviews. Falco's admission that she can experience an emotional universe through her acting, that whilst is fictional can feel like real life, reveals the depth of her ability in not only telling a story, but also in living through it. The strength of Falco's acting ability offers deep resonance to diverse audiences. This book is both an examination of *Nurse Jackie* and an analysis of Edie Falco as an outstanding actress and political figure.

Nurse Jackie was provocative for its focus on the central character of Jackie Peyton played by Falco, who is represented as addicted to prescription drugs, yet is efficient in her role as a nurse, and largely is considered as a valued peer, with almost heroic proportions. Considered part of antihero and quality television, the series was not only highly praised by critics including nominations for 23 Emmys (winning five), but also reached wide audiences, largely enabled through the sophisticated scriptwriting of Liz Brixius and Linda Wallem, and the refined acting performance of Edie Falco in the starring role. The series focus on the opiate addiction in the United States offered a contemporary critical insight into the loss of the American Dream. Central within this is how the series mediates the notion of the addict, as a functioning character attempting to fit in, at the same time exploring aspects of stasis, abjection and alienation.

In researching this book specifically as a gay man, I was interested in how Edie Falco mediates the notion of the other within *Nurse Jackie*. I believe that often we see elements in an actor's potential that might not necessarily represent ourselves directly, but we see personal elements that transgress boundaries of gender or sexuality. Edie Falco's performative potential not only speaks empathetically of the human condition, but also intuitively represents the deepest personal feelings, such as being out of place, not understanding where we fit and intimating our fallibility.

In addition, Falco's work as a political activist concerned for social welfare and social justice are key elements that reveal her integrity as an actress, including her ability to work on small-scale projects, and those that might be seen as collaborative. Falco appears at the centre of *Nurse Jackie* as an enduring iconic inspiration, despite changes in scriptwriting and production management over its duration.

At the same time *Nurse Jackie* offers a critique of healthcare institutions in the United States, including the failure to keep community hospitals open, and how rehabilitation programmes for nurses wishing to return to work could be problematic. This book ultimately frames a call to action (see Conclusion), suggesting that we can better understand the life world of the addict, and put into place processes that might involve institutional change.

Whilst the series is entirely fictional, this book offers scope in making connections to the real world. This might not only be apparent in Falco's history of (alcohol) addiction, and scriptwriters Liz Brixius's and Linda Wallem's experience of prescription drug addiction; I argue that central within this could be the closure of Saint Vincent's Hospital in New York, which is referenced in the last episode of the series, as the fictional hospital of All Saints closes itself. It appears as if the demise of Saint Vincent's Hospital offers a real-world context to the fictional drama series.

The loss of Saint Vincent's Hospital must have been immense for the local community. Historically, it played a fundamental part in leading the response to the HIV/AIDS crisis (New York AIDS Memorial 2018), serving minority groups affected by the disease at that time such as gay men, sex workers, haemophiliacs and drug addicts. This historical connection offers deep resonance for me, as HIV/AIDS activist Pedro Zamora was brought there in 1994 as his life was ending, resulting from symptoms related to the HIV syndrome. I had researched Pedro's life (Pullen 2016b), and whilst he likely caught HIV from unprotected sex, rather than through sharing unclean needles whilst injecting drugs, responses to the person with AIDS as with the drug addict are not that dissimilar. Few people take time to understand the meaning of a person's life that is affected by HIV or drugs, but rather make judgements, considering the pathology and culpability of the individual for getting themselves into this place.

However *Nurse Jackie* suggests that we should not give up on people, largely enabled in the series by real people writing or performing with personal knowledge of addiction, in a manner that is autobiographical. As I have theorised the media performances of activist Pedro Zamora (Pullen 2016b), Liz Brixius, Linda Wallem and Edie Falco, similarly present details of their autobiographical lives with the hope of educating audiences. While despair, dissolution and abjection might frame the addict's life; I argue that it is a mirror of the human condition. We are all frail and transitory beings, influenced not by stability, but an urge to move forward, sometimes down the wrong path but still in the company of ourselves, and others who may find us.

Acknowledgements

I would like to thank Routledge and particularly Felisa Salvago-Keyes for commissioning this book. I would also like to thank Bournemouth University, and particularity Christa van Raalte for supporting this project. Also, I would like to thank Justin Lubin for image permissions. I would like to note the usefulness of the online resource www.springfieldspringfield.co.uk for the provision of *Nurse Jackie* scripts, often making it easy to track the details of a specific episode. Most significantly, I would like to thank my partner Ian Davies, for his inspirational support in the development of this book.

Introduction

Nurse Jackie (2009–15) offers a complex moral universe, where its leading character, Jackie Peyton, is not only represented as an heroic role model and as a valued peer, but also she appears as a compulsive addict and a failing mother. Jackie's moral dilemma is summed up in an exchange with Lily (see Figure 0.1), a young gunshot victim brought to ER with a bullet lodged in her head (Season 2, Ep. 8).[1] After a complex operation, Jackie visits Lily picking up the bullet (which has been saved) and marvels at it:

Lily: That was in my brain, which is fine by the way. . . . You said you were going to be there when I woke up. It was the only reason that I didn't completely lose my shit.

Jackie: I know Honey, and then the day sort of just got away from me. Do you want me to get rid of this for you?

Lily: I want you to hang on to it. Keep your fucking promises!

In what seems like an unusual occurrence for Jackie Peyton, who can usually do her job exceedingly well despite being impaired through addiction to opiate drugs, it is as if Lily can see Jackie's troubling moral universe. *Nurse Jackie* is a provocative television drama that not only frames the life of the addict, but also engages the audience to experience Jackie's feelings, and attempt to understand how she got there, and how she cannot easily escape. The exchange between Lily and Jackie might offer a metaphor for the series; Jackie carries the bullet around with her, as both a signifier of recovery, and that of near death. While the bullet is never seen again after this sequence, our knowledge of her burden, and her unlikeliness to recover, immerses the audience creatively into her private and troubling world.

This book explores the ground-breaking series *Nurse Jackie*, considering not only its narrative meaning, but also places into context diverse cultural engagements. This includes a focus on the significance of the producers,

Figure 0.1 Edie Falco as Jackie Peyton (left) and Justine Cotsonas as Lily (right) in a scene from *Nurse Jackie*: series 2, episode 8.

Showtime, screenshot.

creators and scriptwriters, the generic constitution of the series, the context of female identity within the workplace, the inherent dynamic of its star Edie Falco, its relationship to therapy culture, its reference to failing health-care institutions, its relation to the American Dream, and the epidemic in opiate addiction. At the same time, whilst also framing the significance of quality television and star theory, this book explores the significance of *Oz, The Sopranos, 30 Rock, and Law & Order True Crime: The Menendez Murders* within which Falco has also worked. Additionally, this book examines a range of diverse texts that I argue inform our reading of *Nurse Jackie*, such as *Black Narcissus, Maude, NYPD Blue, Sex and The City, Scrubs, ER* and *House MD*. While these foundational texts offer a diverse range of generic contexts, from films about nuns, to televisions sitcoms, crime drama and hospital drama, and *Nurse Jackie* is the product of diverse individuals, the central focus involves one individual, and relates the significance of New York City.

Nurse Jackie gravitates around the star persona of Edie Falco. Her involvement within the series, I argue, reveals the positive nature of a celebrity culture where therapeutic insight may be offered through self-reflection. As an ex (alcohol) addict herself, Falco presents a nuanced and calibrated performative ability in delivering politicised discourse concerning the life world of the addict, and their social interaction. At the same time, I argue that the series offers a real-life interaction with history in New York, evident in the closure of hospitals there, critiquing institutional and healthcare social commitments. Specifically, I argue that the fictional setting of All Saint's Hospital, and notably its closure and conversion into luxury condominiums reflects the real-life closure of Saint Vincent's Hospital in Greenwich Village, New York. However, the origins of *Nurse Jackie* offers a complex narrative trajectory that frames both the significance of real-life experiences and the need to focus on political ideals.

Origins of *Nurse Jackie*

Notably as Peter Facinelli (who plays Dr "Coop") reports in the DVD documentary *All About Edie* that accompanies the first season of *Nurse Jackie*, that "in the beginning of the series it was titled the *Untitled Edie Falco Show*", framing the significance of Falco in stimulating the drive by Showtime to create a series that centred around her. Despite this, the origins of the series are a little more complex.

Co-creators and scriptwriters of *Nurse Jackie* Liz Brixius and Linda Wallem had a passionate idea, in wanting to create a television drama series that focused on addiction. As recovering prescription drug addicts themselves, they had an innate knowledge of the subject area, and inevitably there was a political desire to tell this story. With this in mind, they had produced a pilot entitled *Insatiable* for Showtime, which incidentally involved the contribution of Peter Facinelli (who later joined the cast of *Nurse Jackie*, as the character of Dr Coop). Although *Insatiable* was not picked up for serial production, Lionsgate had a script on addiction written by Evan Dunsky, entitled *Nurse Mona*. As Edie Falco had expressed interest in potentially working on the project, Showtime asked Brixius and Wallem to rework the script for *Nurse Mona* (with the permission of Dunsky). Brixius tells us that *Nurse Mona* was an entirely different prospect to what *Nurse Jackie* became:

> It would have been an awesome graphic novel. Most of it was in voiceover and parts of it were animated. The doctors were names like Dr Sarcophagus and Dr Mellifluous, and at night they all turned into bats and they hung in the janitor's closet.
>
> (YouTube 2018d)

Offering a focus on the gothic, the metaphysical and the supernatural, the original concept of *Nurse Mona* suggested an essence of what *Nurse Jackie* became.

Edie Falco (ABC 2018) in reading the original script for *Nurse Mona*, advises us that the central "character was similar [to what Jackie Peyton became] she was dark", but also she also had "powers to see auras around people" and "she had a thing where she would keep articles from the people who died, and she also had imaginary people in her life". Hence the original concept of *Nurse Mona*, through its gothic approach, seemed to offer great potential, and I argue that elements of the original script potentially remain in *Nurse Jackie*'s use of the chapel at the hospital as a contemplative metaphysical space (see Figure 0.2). However in *Nurse Mona*'s focus on the supernatural and the macabre, it may have not been appealing to mainstream audiences.

Despite this Edie Falco saw merit in the concept of *Nurse Mona*, but wanted to more centrally focus on the narrative of addiction, which was less prominent in the original draft. She confirms a particular political approach in agreeing to do the series, with regards to the representation of drug addiction:

> The one thing that I requested is that it be done realistically that it has ramifications, as it does, and we can't "TV-ise" her relationship to drugs, and everything turns out fine.
>
> (ABC 2018)

Hence Edie Falco played a central role in the development of the series, alongside Dunsky who created the original concept, and Brixius and Wallem who adapted and more fully formed the series.

While some might argue that the original concept of *Nurse Mona* might have made a great original television drama, the influence of Edie Falco,

Figure 0.2 Edie Falco as Jackie Peyton in the chapel at All Saint's Hospital in *Nurse Jackie*.

Showtime, screenshot.

alongside the experience of Brixius and Wallem, stimulated the formation of something more mainstream that could reach wider audiences, but was highly politically charged in its representation of drug addiction.

Reception, Endurance and Controversy

Nurse Jackie, originally broadcast on Showtime over seven seasons between June 8, 2009 and June 25, 2015, has received high profile attention, including frequent nominations and actual awards. The series overall was nominated 23 times for Emmys winning five of these, and was nominated five times both by the Golden Globes and the Screen Actors Guild. Notable moments include when Edie Falco won an Emmy as outstanding lead actress for the series in 2010, and was also nominated five successive times after this (2011–15). Merritt Weaver (who plays Zoey) also won an Emmy as outstanding supporting actress in 2013.[2]

Although the series has been praised by a number of media critics (Beck 2012; Gorton 2016; Nemeth 2011), and the series has achieved longstanding success, enduring for seven seasons from 2009 to 2015, at the same time responses from health professions were more ambiguous. For example, the American Nurses Association reported that *Nurse Jackie*'s portrayal of health professionals who violate the Code of Ethics involving "on-the-job drug use to inappropriate nurse/patient contact" (cited in Nemeth 2011, p. 9) might have a lasting negative impact. While conversely, The Truth about Nursing (2018) awards gave *Nurse Jackie* its top award for best portrayal, because:

> New York ED nurse Jackie Peyton remained a tough clinical virtuoso who used creative and effective ways to help patients lead better lives or/and lasting peace, despite her own ethical and personal issues.

Added to this as Hirt, Wong, Erichsen and White (2013) report in *The Media Teacher*, a specialist educational journal, the usefulness of the series, may be appreciated in context:

> *Nurse Jackie* is heavy with ethical dilemmas, communication issues and patient advocacy. . . . This dark comedy has a refreshing take on the medical drama, and its clips could be very effective in a teaching session, with appropriate debriefing.
>
> (p. 241)

Despite this, I would argue that *Nurse Jackie* offers a very profound philosophical and educational value, evident in the series focus on addiction as much as practice within healthcare.

As Sam Quinones (2016) reports concerning America's opiate epidemic, and the loss of the American Dream, it extends from increased marketing, availability and the transformation of high level opiate-based painkillers such as MS Contin (to OxyContin), which were previously reserved for recovery from surgery and end-of-life pain care, but are now more widely available, and abused. *Nurse Jackie* offers a refreshing if not shocking expose on this subject, employing the domestic medium of television to address families at home.

However *Nurse Jackie* follows an increasing emergence of drug representation on TV.[3] As Christenson et al. (2000) report exploring American television: "Illicit drugs were infrequently mentioned and rarely shown in primetime television. In the few episodes that portrayed illicit drug use, nearly all showed negative consequences. Typically, major characters were not shown using illicit drugs or communicating pro-use statements" (p. 3). However as Paul Manning (2015) reports:

> From the mid-1990s onward, drug use began to be understood in television drama as part of the fabric of everyday life, as a backdrop against which the more important business of plots quite unrelated to drug use would play out.
>
> (p. 49)

For example in 1993, UK television company Channel 4 produced *Tales of the City* set in San Francisco, which prominently features the representation of recreational drugs such as Quaaludes and marijuana, in a popular adaptation of Armistead Maupin's original book. Later in the UK the social realist comedy drama *Shameless* (2004–13) and the youth culture coming-of-age drama *Skins* (2007–13) both featured drug use as part of everyday life, within diverse class and community settings. Added to this Manning points out that mainstream US shows such as *Desperate Housewives*, *Sex and the City* and *Ugly Betty* "permitted fleeting glimpses of normalized, non-pathological soft drug use" (p. 49), leading to more explicit representations within *The Wire*, *Weeds*, *Breaking Bad* and *Nurse Jackie*.

While in terms of regulation it is important to note that the broadcast of *Nurse Jackie* on Showtime, a premium cable channel is not subject to the broadcasting regulations of the FCC (2018) in the United States (Butler 2018); inevitably when broadcast on network or terrestrial television, regulations do apply. For example when *Nurse Jackie* was first broadcast in the United Kingdom it appeared on the terrestrial station BBC 2, and consequently was subject to the regulation of Ofcom (2018).[4] As such *Nurse Jackie* is a creative text, which is not only provocative and challenging and designed for premium cable audiences, but also is suitable for mainstream audiences. As Manning states, "*Nurse Jackie* reminds us that the pharmaceutical technologies developed to relieve pain and sooth the modern psyche have potentially destructive consequences" (p. 49), offering an important accessible educational stance.

Despite this as *Nurse Jackie* developed over the years, originally under the leadership of Liz Brixius and Linda Wallem from series 1 to 4, and then later under that of Clyde Phillips from series 5 to 7, some commentators have criticised its transformation. In a provocative article entitled *When Bad Things Happen to Good TV Shows* by Martha P. Nochimson (2018), she tells us:

> Brixius, Dunsky and Wallem originally created a universe of inde-terminate enigmas; Phillips [developed the series] into something approaching a medical procedural, a universe with hard, clean edges, rigidly designed resolution, and hard and fast judgements.

Although after the arrival of Phillips, the tone of the series changed, offer-ing a more obvious connection to regular medical dramas, such as including more obvious romantic/sexual narratives, including those between Zoey and Dr Ike Prentice, and between Dr Coop and Dr Roman, I argue that the produc-ers probably developed these narratives as counterpoint relief to the increas-ing trauma that Jackie Peyton is going through. Although the early direction of Brixius and Wallem was exceptional, and probably more nuanced, I argue that Phillips brought a much-needed visceral edge in the representation of Jackie's dilemmas, mediating the appropriate psychological universe.

Despite this, as Brixius and Wallem parted and Phillips arrived, the long-standing presence of Edie Falco, in many ways at the helm of the series for its entire endurance, ensured its integrity, realism and veracity.

The Sopranos Affect

Specifically, Falco's representation within *The Sopranos* informs the audi-ences reading of *Nurse Jackie*. Whilst later in Chapter 3, I more fully con-sider her potential in the series in relation to her star persona; it is worth considering a key moment in *The Sopranos*, which I argue stimulates an affective emotional depth that may inform our understanding of Edie Falco in playing Jackie Peyton in *Nurse Jackie*.

Edie Falco, in a detailed and lengthy interview with the Archive of Ameri-can Television (AAT 2018), mentions a key episode in *The Sopranos* that she enjoyed acting in and thought was engaging. In the final season, in a pivotal episode entitled "Cold Stones", Falco playing the role of Carmela Soprano, visits Paris with female friend Rosalie. Whilst back in New York, the usual Mafia business takes place, including two brutal murders of Mafia mem-bers themselves, Carmela reflects on the different social and artistic world in Paris. In a key sequence Carmela and Rosalie wander across the Alexander

III bridge, with Carmela instinctively saying "Who could have built this?", whilst she finds pleasure and awe in looking at the ornate statues there. Later after visiting the cathedral of St Eustache, and now in a restaurant, Carmela in conversation with Rosalie, reflects on the meaning of their visit:

> When you go to a place you've never been before it's like all the people are imaginary until you got there. It's like until you saw them, they never existed, and you never existed to them. . . . It's the same as when you die. Life goes on without you. Like it does in Paris when we are not here.

Falco in the role of Carmela provides a deeply moving scene, offering an existential discourse. In finding time away from her life back in New York, Carmela seems to take time out to reflect on the meaning of life, and of travel. Significantly, the way she engages with the art (on the bridge and in the Louvre) presents an innocent playfulness that we know is hard to believe, as back home the murderous routines of the Mafia continue. This juxtaposition between life, pleasure and death, and that of freedom, indulgence and innocence, offers an engaging prospect. This is specifically apparent in Falco's nuanced rendition (see Chapter 3) of the character of Carmela Soprano, seeming both as an innocent abroad, and as a responsible mother at home. This vision of Carmela, as a sentient being, but also knowingly culpable, I argue informs our reading of Jackie Peyton. Carmela offers a premonition of what Jackie Peyton became, evident in her relationship to morality, mortality and emotions, taking time to discover the meaning of her life, all the while making compromises. As Amy Raphael (2018) reports in *The Guardian* in comparing Falco's work in both *The Sopranos* and *Nurse Jackie*, "Both Carmela and Jackie are emotionally flawed characters and it's their very vulnerability that makes them so appealing".

Falco's nuanced representation of Jackie Peyton, informed by her previous representation of Carmela in *The Sopranos*, at the same time keying into her own experience of (alcohol) addiction, offers a nuanced performative potential that I argue stimulates endurance.

After *Nurse Jackie* and Edie Falco's Activism

After the final episode of *Nurse Jackie*, *The Hollywood Reporter* asked Clyde Phillips what legacy did he think the series would leave behind. His response was simple:

> That you can love a flawed person—because we are all flawed. Beyond that, an understanding of what it's like to be an addict, to be in love with an addict, and to be friends with and trust an addict.

Suggesting that audiences might begin to understand the life world of the addict, Phillips frames the problem of the addict in society. In contrast when Edie Falco was asked the same question, of the legacy of *Nurse Jackie*, she offers a more abstract answer:

> I don't know we are in a funny time with these Anti-hero [shows]. . . . You find yourself having feelings for a person, albeit a pretend one, who does bad things, and makes bad choices. And maybe there is something in that that everybody wants to feel like they are in fact a member of the human race. . . . This isn't *Father Knows Best*, this is *Breaking Bad*. . . . And watching the ramifications unfold we get to experience life as it is now.

(AAT 2018)

Offering a more personal, almost viewer-like response, it is clear that Falco doesn't want to aggrandise the impact of the show. Rather she offers an experiential response that juxtaposes other texts, the family-oriented sitcom *Father Knows Best*, and the progressive drug addiction drama *Breaking Bad*.

Despite this, Edie Falco's earnest and modest response on the meaning of the show is quite fitting. Seeming like an audience member, rather than an important actress, she reaches out in a human way, framing the significance of emotions, in accepting the human condition, and by token a "call to action", advocating understanding. Part of this work involves a collaborative nature.

After *Nurse Jackie* Falco went to work on various projects, such as the high profile series *Law & Order True Crime: The Menendez Murders* (discussed in Chapter 3), also involving herself in more modest projects. Notably she worked on *Horace and Pete*, an independent production, created, written and directed by Louis CK. Playing the role of the older sister Sylvia to the main cast member Horace, she is represented in this social realist comedy drama as having cancer, desiring that her brother sell the family bar to pay for her chemotherapy. Produced on a small budget, and only available online through subscription from Louis CK (see Louis CK 2018), a sense of community and grass roots is presented.

Additionally a sense of introspection and artistry is also apparent in Falco starring alongside Jay Duplass in the independent film *Outside In* (2017), scripted by Duplass with Lynn Shelton. Offering a provocative narrative of a teacher who develops a close relationship with a former student who is now an ex convict, a sense of progressive social realism is presented, in framing the human condition. At the same time, this integrates with Jay Duplass's "troubled" identity within the progressive drama series *Transparent* (2104–) where he plays an adult who still bears the pain of sexual abuse as a child. Falco, with Duplass, offers a deep sense of painful emotional union in *Outside In*, framing the complexity of age-different relationships.

Such a sense of union is also apparent where Falco reports in the online video blog Talk Stoop (YouTube 2018g) of her passion for the 52nd Street Project, telling us:

> little Hells Kitchen kids write plays, and adults act them out. And these kids, their lives are being changed, by participating in this organisation. From beginning to end, it's a real success story, in a culture right now when there are not so many of them.

Referencing her modest participation, advising that this year she will "probably be playing a broccoli", she reflects a changing political landscape in the United States, and her investment in supporting social care.

Whilst Falco has moved on from *Nurse Jackie*, it is clear that her realist and experiential approach to the series is contextual to her life work as an actress and political activist. This is particularly evident in her support for the Democratic party, apparent in her voiceover contribution to the Lulu Land Creative resistance video (Creative Resistance 2018). In this video she relates a need for "universal single payer healthcare", "fully funded public schools", "strong environmental safeguards" and "sanctuary state legislation to protect all immigrants", framing a need to resist the influence of President Trump, and the Republican party. In a shaming, and to a degree ironic performance, Falco highlights the proclivity for New Yorkers to vote Democrat, but that a small group of politicians under the umbrella of the "Independent Democrat Conference" have splintered the Democrat vote, enabling the Republicans to resist the social measures that are ideals for Democrat voters. Offering a parody to the film *La La Land* (2016), in the campaign's title "Lulu Land", Falco's star identity is referenced, at the same time parodying the idea of cultural and social oblivion.

Falco's star persona offers insight in mediating a social realist narrative, also engaging with the ideologies of social welfare and social justice. Whilst *Nurse Jackie* may be less explicit in attempting to convey the life world of the addict to mainstream audiences, I nevertheless argue that this is deeply resonant. As we shall see in considering the structure of this book, Edie Falco's role is central in mediating the meaning of the series.

Structure of the Book

Chapter 1 considers the generic context of *Nurse Jackie*, examining both the notion of "body trauma TV" (Jacobs 2003) and "heroine television" (Brunsdon 1997, p. 34). At the same time the context of the female nurse is explored, framing earlier representations, such as in *ER* and *House MD*. With a central focus on soap opera contexts, and female workplace identity within the setting of New York City, earlier influential texts are examined such as *Maude*, *Rhoda*, *NYPD Blue* and *Sex and the City*.

Chapter 2 explores the significance of quality television, and that of situation comedy, in defining *Nurse Jackie*'s relationship to the American Dream, and the context of opiate addiction. Whilst framing the notion of the absent and unstable mother, this chapter offers close textual analysis on Jackie Peyton's interaction with family. At the same time, it places into context the political vision of the series, evident in *Nurse Jackie*'s ability to explore the challenge of the addict's life.

Chapter 3 explores Edie Falco's star persona, considering the development of her career, looking both at prior texts such as *Oz*, *The Sopranos* and *30 Rock*, alongside more recent work (since *Nurse Jackie*) such as *Law & Order True Crime: The Menendez Murders*. As part of this, I explore the performative nature of Falco's persona, not only discussing her nuanced and calibrated acting style, but also examining her politicised "autobiographical self" (Pullen 2016b).

Chapter 4 considers the notion of heroism and morality, examining the representational world of the series with reference to desire and the will to be good. Framing the foundational significance of films that represent nuns as spiritual heroes such as in *Black Narcissus* and *Agnes of God*, an intertextual examination takes place, foregrounding the significance of "the moral imaginary" (Dant 2012). As part of this, female heroism is discussed, framing the significance of understanding the world, rather than following the right path.

Chapter 5 examines the significance of therapy culture in our reading of *Nurse Jackie*. Whilst also exploring the life world of the addict, this chapter frames the impact and meaning of trauma and woundedness. In doing this a central point of concern is that *Nurse Jackie* critiques the failings of institutions evident in hospital closures, such as Saint Vincent's Hospital in Greenwich Village, New York, and the wider treatment of nurses and the rehab Diversion programme, in framing the narrative of the addict.

Conclusion

While Jackie Peyton and All Saints Hospital are fictional elements in *Nurse Jackie*, the presence of Edie Falco and the memory of Saint Vincent's Hospital persist as real-life iconic signifiers. While neither Jackie Peyton and Edie Falco, nor All Saints Hospital and Saint Vincent's Hospital are inherently entwined, a sense of realism is offered in our knowledge of their possible connection. Edie Falco has a life history as a recovering (alcohol) addict, and Saint Vincent's Hospital went bankrupt, and was potentially the inspiration for the ending of the fictional All Saint's Hospital. The audience's identification with an actress who is not only incredibly skilled, but also has experienced the life world of the addict, alongside New York's identification with a valued healthcare institution that is no longer is there, offers great resonance.

Nurse Jackie critiques a failing social and institutional world, through relating the personal to the institutional, and the culturally oppressive. In a similar manner that Edie Falco in the Lulu Land video (discussed above) asks the Democrats to consider where their allegiances lie with regards to social welfare and social justice, *Nurse Jackie* offers up a site of identification, to test our respect for others, suggesting a call to action (see Conclusion). Whether we identify with the real life person Edie Falco or the fictional character of Jackie Peyton, or the scriptwriters and producers such as Liz Brixius and Linda Wallem, or Clyde Phillips, our focus is drawn to the narrative of the addict, and how we may try to understand our own experience, or even those of others. As part therapy culture, but also part of entertainment culture, it is easy to move on now the series has ended, failing to acknowledge the humanity of the addict as a reflection of ourselves.

Nurse Jackie may have ended, and if Edie Falco has anything to do with it, there will not be a sequel, as she is determined that the audience understand the ramifications of addiction, that if an individual fails to meaningfully try to keep on living, this will expedite an early ending.

However as this book reveals, even if something has ended, it potentially remains in our psyche for some time, if not forever. In the manner that Edie Falco, in the guise of Carmela in *The Sopranos*, reflects upon the meaning of life in Paris walking around the ruins at Musée de Cluny, and touches the ancient foundations (see Figure 0.3) (in the episode "Cold Stones", discussed above):

> The city is so old, to think about all the people who have lived here, generation after generation, hundreds and hundreds of years, all those lives. . . . It makes you look at yourself differently.

Nurse Jackie makes you look at yourself differently. It does this not by glamorising or even judging the addict's life, it places you in context. We are like Carmela, in a different country, within the ruins of an ancient city, hoping to find a way back home, but also hoping that this moment might gain us some deeper understanding. Addictive behaviour in its many different forms can be part of the human condition, which is often in itself beyond our understanding. Comprehension comes not from understanding, but rather in considering the ephemeral nature of human existence and the fallibility

Figure 0.3 Edie Falco as Carmela Soprano in *The Sopranos* at Musée De Cluny, Paris, in a scene from series 6, episode 11 "Cold Stones".
HBO, screenshot.

of individuals, including ourselves among this number. In the manner that Jackie Peyton holds the philosophical bullet as a reminder of her constant near death experience and of potential recovery (as discussed above), we are all part of this continuum, needing not so much to understand our pathology, but that we are not inherently alone.

Notes

1. See *Nurse Jackie* Episode Index with credits for scriptwriters and directors, later in this book.
2. Besides this Falco was nominated for four Golden Globes as best actress (2010, 2011, 2014 and 2015), and was also nominated four times by the Screen Actors Guild for outstanding performance (2010–2013). Added to this, Lisa Coleman and Wendy Melvoin won an Emmy for outstanding main title theme in 2010, and Jan McLaughlin and Peter Waggoner won two Emmys for outstanding sound mixing for in 2013 and 2014.
3. It is important to note that the representation of drugs within film clearly has been influential, on those within television. This includes *Trainspotting* (1996) and *Requiem for a Dream* (2000), which similar to *Nurse Jackie* represents domestic and everyday drug usage (see Manning 2015 and Moreno 2009).
4. *Nurse Jackie* was first broadcast on terrestrial TV on BBC 2, on January 4, 2010, later transferring from season 3 to the satellite station Sky Atlantic on July 5, 2011.

1 Female Work and Hospital Drama

Introduction

In the closing episode of season 6 of *Nurse Jackie*, Jackie Peyton is represented as on the run, travelling on the motorway to the airport, likely to be found out for illegally using a doctor's identity to obtain drugs and falsifying a patient's personal security card to cover her tracks. However her escape is held up en route when she administers life-saving support to a dying patient who is the victim of a car crash, later accidentally crashing her own car and is alerted to the police.

All the while her journey of escape had not been to find an easier and safer life, but it had been to follow "a cause", to offer her services as a nurse to the victims of a local flood disaster in Florida. Jackie Peyton is represented as committed to her work ethic even in times of flight and likely incarceration. The notion of work informs her "life blood" and identity, where she seemingly cannot exist unless she performs her function as a nurse.

This chapter consequently places into context the narrative drive of *Nurse Jackie*, which I argue frames the significance of labour and workplace identity. At the same time I discuss audience identification with female characters in soap opera, considering the significance of irony and ambivalence in assessing the narrative potential. As part of this, I argue that the generic constitution of *Nurse Jackie* is both medical drama and "heroine television".

Medical Drama and Heroism Television

Jason Jacobs (2003) tells us in his ground-breaking book *Body Trauma TV: The New Hospital Dramas*:

> Hospital dramas of the 1970s, included frequent explicitness in the discussion of medical and social "problems": abortion, homosexuality, rape, drug addiction, artificial insemination, venereal disease, issues

that had been more or less excluded from the earlier shows on the grounds of taste and audience sensitivity.

(p. 7)

Revealing a new kind of realism and a shift towards cultural liberation, Jacobs highlights the significance of hospital drama for its ability to focus on minority identity issues and the situation of the other in society.

At the same time Charlotte Brunsdon (1997) considers the notion of "heroine television" as occurring in a range of television dramas including sitcom and crime drama, featuring exemplars as *I Love Lucy* (1951–57), *The Mary Tyler Moore Show* (1970–77), *The Golden Girls* (1985–92), *Cagney and Lacey* (1981–88) and *Prime Suspect* (1991–2006). Brunsdon tells us:

> "Heroine Television" is centrally about female characters living their lives, usually working both inside and outside the home, usually not in permanent relationships with men, sometimes with children, and trying to cope. . . . [T]hese shows are all in some fundamental way, addressing feminism, or addressing their gender that feminism has made public about the contradictory demands on women.

(p. 34)

Brunsdon reflects the significance of television programming that features females as central characters and lead storytellers, seeming to offer a sense of political activism, and identification for audiences.

In this sense both the notion of hospital drama as a genre, and the significance of female-focused television dramas within diverse genres, informs our reading of *Nurse Jackie*. Jacobs highlights hospital drama for its ability to map "societal anxieties on to the body . . . as a site for the application of benevolent medical science [framing] [i]llness and injury [as] the catalysts for the exploration of human relationships, emotions, desires and morals" (p. 7). Brunsdon highlights the importance of positive role models for female audiences, framing the significance of "feminist textual analysis" and its focus on two types of programmes, "those addressed to women and those centrally about women characters" (p. 34). *Nurse Jackie* is situated as part of the genre of hospital drama, and independently may be considered as an exemplar of "heroine television".

Although the constitution of "heroism" may be complex in *Nurse Jackie*, as in many ways she is an "anti-heroine" (see Buonnanno [2017] and Chapter 3) and consequently could be seen as counter productive in advancing a positive sense of feminism, it is this balance between the generic progression of hospital drama and its relationship to female identity that is central. In many ways it is possible to argue that although hospital drama has for many years focused on women, including representations of many female characters, largely it has (to paraphrase Brunsdon) "addressed women" audiences, rather than necessarily "been about women characters".

Within hospital drama, there is a dominance of the male lead character evident in the identity of the doctor, and this is counterpointed with the role of the nurse, who normally takes a subordinate role. Despite this, a female audience could be addressed not only in representing the nurses as able and inspirational supporters of the diagnosis of the doctor, but also in framing the notion of the domestic narrative, including romance narratives. While there may be a the tension between the role of the nurse and the doctor evident in series such as *The Nurses* (1962–65), *Marcus Welby MD* (1967–75), *M*A*S*H* (1972–83), *St. Elsewhere* (1982–88), *ER* (1994–2009), *Scrubs* (2001–10), *Grey's Anatomy* (2005–) and *House MD* (2004–12), often nurses are represented as central storytellers, who not only care for the patients in an environment away from home, but also replicate the traditional domestic and romance narrative that centres on male and female dynamics.

As Luke Hockley and Leslie Gardner (2011) tell us discussing the context of *House MD* and its precursors within the genre, "These programs were often headed by a patrician figure such as the senior doctor in *Marcus Welby MD*. . . . The subversion of this particular trope is one of the familiar views of *House*, whose central character had a bedside manner that is somewhat different to that of the kindly Dr Welby" (pp. 1–2). While the male lead in *House* subverts the traditional relationship between male professionals within the medical world, the doctor is nevertheless considered as the leading authority, and primarily the hero, who potentially subordinates females. For example in *House*, although the lead doctor (played by Hugh Laurie) is unconventional, his interactions with female members of staff (and patients) reference the regular "masculine-active" and "feminine-passive" dynamic. For example, when House initially assesses his new medical team (in season 1), which includes a strong willed and talented female doctor, Dr Allison Cameron, he openly admits that he recruited her as she is good-looking. However he states that his would be a trial for her to advance within the medical profession, because she would have been stereotyped for her good looks. Hence he hires her, as she must be a great doctor, because she has advanced despite herself. Hence even in *House*, a hospital drama that is progressive in terms of defining the doctor as "wounded" (he is disabled, evident in a leg injury) and consequently must be "human", the masculine order is maintained, or at least referenced.

Nurse Jackie offers a complex prospect in this dynamic. Although Jackie Peyton performs the role of the nurse as subordinate to the doctor, in effect she challenges this hierarchy. For example, in the pilot episode of the series Jackie Peyton and junior Dr "Coop" care for a bike messenger who arrives at the emergency department and has received head trauma. After Jackie Peyton raises medical procedural concerns, which are ignored (or devalued) by Coop, the patient dies. In a scene where both characters stand in the presence of the now deceased young man, Jackie acts more like a doctor than a nurse, admonishing Coop, that:

> I had to sit there and look that kid's mother in the eye and tell her that we did everything that we could. You dumb shit—that was my patient! I told you he was slipping and he was. If I tell you to order a scan you order a Goddamn scan, because if you don't I will go to the next doctor and the next doctor after that. In the meantime that kid died, and it is all on you.

Seeming more like a doctor rather than a nurse, the doctor/nurse dynamic is inverted. The fictional female character of Jackie Peyton takes the lead in what might be termed as having insight in the best "procedural practice" within the medical profession. In this sense Jackie, as a female and not even a doctor, challenges the primacy of the male doctor in following best practice. Such a focus on mortality in relation to practice is central in highlighting the significance of audience engagement.

As Jason Jacobs (2003) discusses in relation to the drama *ER*:

> The death of a patient is the pretext for discussion about procedure so that ethical issues are framed within the specific context of working practices. Viewer proximity is distributed between our sympathy for the dead patient and [the health professional's] experienced emotional response to it.
>
> (p. 3)

In this sense our understanding of the medical treatment of the patient, in context with the professional and the emotional universe of the characters, offers a framework of identification for the audience. Jackie Peyton's commentary that the doctor did not follow her best practice recommendations, evident in the death of the bike messenger, challenges the patriarchal narrative conventions of hospital drama, through framing the authoritative voice of the nurse rather than the doctor.

As Jacobs tells us, historically

> [r]eassurance as personified in the figure of the infallible, capable doctor and in the early shows [such as *Medic* (1954–55) and *Dr Kildare* (1961–66) prioritise] the individual doctor's central role in healing people; typically the doctors were white males at the centre of authority in the hospital or practice.
>
> (p. 5)

Contemporary hospital dramas featuring ensemble casts with doctors and nurses such as in *St. Elsewhere* (1982–88), *ER* and *Grey's Anatomy*, often frame incidences where nurses save the lives of patients presenting superior knowledge to doctors. However in *Nurse Jackie*, it is the focus on the emotional as much as the procedural that prioritises a heroic female identity.

I argue that *Nurse Jackie* complicates historical notions of hospital drama, not only seeming as part of "heroism television" (Brunsdon 1997), but also in doing so presents new scope within the procedural and the pathological, through framing the female nurse as authority. As Jason Jacobs advises us, hospital dramas or "body trauma TV" may defined within these contexts/eras:

- Paternal (mid 1950s–late 1960s)—where male doctors were central storytellers, and there is a reverence for best practice.
- Conflict (late 1960s–early 1990s)—where challenges to order were presented in following the youth and liberation movements.
- Apocalypse (early 1990s–early 2000s)—where teams of medical staff work within oppressed social conditions, and there is new realism that accepts mortality.

While it is not simple to map a range of programmes that fit easily within these contexts/eras, it is possible to argue that *Nurse Jackie* is an extension of Jacobs's "Apocalypse" context/era. However rather than a team focus on "rawness, explicitness, pace, cynicism and despair that was effectively normalised in their narratives" (p. 11), the individual personal struggle of the health professional becomes a central narrative trope.

Viewed in this way, *Nurse Jackie* could be considered as a progression of *House*. Both Gregory House, MD (played by Hugh Laurie) and Jackie Peyton (played by Edie Falco), are wounded themselves and are addicted to opioid narcotic medications: House struggles with a leg injury, and openly takes the painkiller Vicodin, and Peyton responded to psychological stress surrounding her identification with her daughter as a child, and became covertly addicted to Percocet/OxyContin (Season 4, Ep. 2). The interrelation of the shows may be evident where both series involve a focus on the procedural and the pathological, albeit in entirely different ways.

Although House is the central medical practitioner, the narrative is less about his personal struggle with addiction (although as the series develops we discover detail of his injury and wider life story), and more about his struggle to diagnose, involving a challenge to the norms of medical practice. For example in the pilot episode of *House*, the narrative of pathology involves his need to solve the case of a woman who seems to exhibit the signs of a brain tumour, but later is revealed to be caused by a parasite. The mystery and cause of this illness is resolved, revealing unconventional medical practice, including House encouraging his medical team to break into the home of the patient, to try and find evidence as to what could be the case of the illness. When pork is found in the refrigerator, a seemingly tenuous link is discovered which leads House to consider that the patient may have consumed pork in South America, where a rare parasite may be found in the meat. While we are not provided with a wider reason why House is in pain, or why he is addicted to painkillers, we witness his excellent skills in deduction and knowledge of medical practice.

In contrast, within the pilot episode of *Nurse Jackie*, we are immediately given access to the imagined psyche of Jackie Peyton. Our first glimpse of Jackie is one of an imaginary death. The camera focuses on a close up of a blurred eye seeming like the moment of death, or the moment when you lose consciousness or experience the effects of drugs. The camera later pans across an empty hospital bathroom floor, revealing Jackie Peyton on the floor flat on her back as if just tripped up, coded by the chewing gum viewed on her shoe.

The music that accompanies this is k.d. lang singing the theme tune to *The Valley of the Dolls*. The use of this song originally composed in 1967 (and sung by Diane Warwick), a tale of female struggle in the entertainment industry and the lure of recreational drugs to aid your career, eventually leading to relationship breakdown and self-effacement, is significant. The lyrics not only frame the impossibility of leaving, or changing direction, but also the mise en scène a 1960s-style hospital room with Peyton herself dressed in white nurse's uniform represent a sense of past. Such a representation suggests that she is living in an imaginary past, that the audience will have little access to, as the series is set in the present day. This is also apparent in using the k.d. lang version of the song rather than the Dionne Warwick version, as if producing a hybridised representation, complicating past and present references. In this sense a fantasy sequence is presented, which I argue reveals her seemingly inaccessible dreams, or nightmares. Added to this we hear a voiceover from *Nurse Jackie*:

> "Let us go then, you and I, when the evening is spread out against the sky like a patient etherized upon a table": T.S. Eliot, 10th grade English, Sister Jane de Chanteau. What a champ. She told me that the people with the greatest capacity for good are the ones with the greatest capacity for evil. Smart fucking nun.

Jackie presents herself as a liminal object between places, time frames and fixed cultural references. As Martha P. Nochimson (2018) observes in reading this scene, Jackie

> isn't going anywhere. She is in a sea of liminality. It isn't purely Jackie's pathology; it is also a cultural pathology. Jackie is addicted to painkillers to keep up the economic and professional demands on her the world she lives in is a mass of contradictions.

Jackie is presented as trapped within the economic and cultural confines of her role as a nurse, only able to do her job through drug addiction. Her focus on procedure relates to her emotional universe, at the same time the audience's attention is drawn to pathology, continually questioning the reasons for her opiate addiction.

Like Gregory House she is skilled in caring for patients, to the extent where she has achieved the highest level of professional ability, which includes instinct and intuition at pathology in determining the best procedures. However unlike House she is a subject trapped in liminality, between the dream world nightmare of her addiction and the demands of her job, encouraging the audience to understand the pathology of Jackie Peyton herself. Asking questions: How did she become addicted? How can she recover from addiction? How will she perform within the workplace? How can she function as a human being?

In this sense while *House* and *Nurse Jackie* both foreground central characters who present a personal drive towards pathology and procedural professionalism or efficiency, they offer different approaches. While *House* is largely concerned for the pathology of disease and illness outside himself, *Nurse Jackie* focuses on self-knowledge in attempting to hold on to her role as a professional health worker and the trial of human fallibility. Such a focus on the "professional self", seeming part of "heroine television", frames female identity as contextual to the workplace, particularly for *Nurse Jackie* within the setting of New York.

Work, Individualisation and New York

The setting of the fictional All Saints Hospital in New York is significant in reading the generic property of the series. Within television and film, real-life hospitals offer an important representational source, for imagination and narrative development. Notably as James Sanders (2001) reports in *Celluloid Skyline: New York and the Movies*, when Universal released *The Seeping City* (1950) using the real-life location of Bellevue Hospital:

> The film offered audiences an extensive tour of the hospital's ageing plant, turn of the century congeries of structures . . . that provided a superbly atmospheric setting for the film's tale of a narcotic ring operating within the hospital walls.
>
> (p. 401)

Utilising the atmosphere and iconography of Bellevue, *The Sleeping City* framed the identity of the ageing historical structure as a setting for narrative development, evoking the real and the mythic city. However, I argue that All

Saints Hospital in *Nurse Jackie* might in fact be based upon St Vincent's Hospital rather than Bellevue, particularly with regards to St Vincent's closure and conversion into luxury condominiums and protests against this in the manner that is represented in *Nurse Jackie* with regards to All Saints (see Figure 1.1 and Chapter 5).[1] The use of film or television "provides a fascinating mirror to the real city, [framing] its waves of immigration, growth, decline, rebirth. . . . The real and mythic cities will intertwine, become entangled, just as they often do in our memory" (Sanders 2001, p. 4).

In *Nurse Jackie*, the notion of the hospital within the city follows a range of television dramas that have explored the significance of females working in municipal roles set in New York. As part of this, series such as *Maude* (1972), *Rhoda* (1978), *Cagney & Lacey* (1981–88), *NYPD Blue* (1993–2003), *Sex and The City* (1998–2004), and *The Sopranos* (1999–2007), relate key feminist narratives connected to the setting of New York City. Central within this is a consideration of the usefulness of female labour within the city, with women often working within municipal roles, or at least roles connected to production, as for example working in offices, retail or the service industry, or maintaining the family household. While reflecting diverse genres with diverse industry contexts, I argue that these shows offer a generic context for the emergence of *Nurse Jackie*.

Figure 1.1 The Fictional Setting of All Saints Hospital as depicted in series 7 of *Nurse Jackie*, with Merritt Weaver as Zoey (left) leading a demonstration against its impending closure. Edie Falco as Jackie Peyton is also featured (centre, with head bowed), alongside Stephen Wallem as Thor Lundgren (to her left).

Showtime, screenshot.

For example in *Maude* and the *Sopranos*, largely we are presented with women who maintain the household. In *Maude* we are presented with Maude Findlay (played by Bea Arthur) who within a pivotal episode must decide whether to have an abortion at aged 47, and within the *Sopranos* we are presented with Carmela Soprano (played by Edie Falco) who maintains her family household despite her husband running the local Mafia. In both these texts, there is the focus on work, and the potential to face up to the demands of modern life in maintaining a sense of usefulness. This I argue relates to the significance of work, as a means to affirm identity.

As Beverley Skeggs and Helen Wood (2012) tell us, "performing work is . . . always about *becoming*, not just *being*; developing potential that is always future directed" (p. 188). Hence the representation of work or labour within television drama connects to a wider concept of future intents and achievement as much as maintenance, and reflecting the established order. Where the producers of *Maude* represent an older woman making a difficult decision about bearing a child, and the producers of the *Sopranos* reveal the ability of a woman to hold a traditional family together despite her family income gained from crime, this reveals a sense of resolve within personal identity to become or maintain a sense of self, despite adversity, or challenges to order.

At the same time a sense of *becoming* as much as *being* is evident where increasingly workplace identity offers a sense of exchange or equality. As Stuart Hall (1998) advises us: "not since the workhouse has Labour been so fervently and single-mindedly valorised" (p. 83). Reflecting the rise of neoliberalism (Saad-Filho and Johnson 2005) where market economies are central in assessing the use and exchange value of individual worker's contributions, increasingly individuals are encouraged to compete with each other in a workplace environment. Central within this is the notion of "individualisation". As Ulrich Beck and Elizabeth Beck-Gernsheim (2002) affirm:

> [I]n modern societies new demand, controls and constraints are being imposed on individuals. Through the job market, the welfare state at institutions, people are tied into a network of regulations, conditions, provisos. . . . The decisive feature of these modern regulations or guidelines is that, far more than earlier, individuals must, in part, supply them for themselves, import them into their biographies through their own actions.
>
> (p. 2)

Nurse Jackie reflects the demand of new controls on the individual, that in many senses require the individuals to work for themselves, in defining how they fit within this new regulatory order. Hence while the role of the nurse still involves adherence to guidelines, professionalism and regulations, increasingly in contemporary society through the demands of competition, workplace hours are extended, pay is reduced and the hierarchical form of the job changes. Rather than fitting into an ordered workplace universe, individuals need to compete with each other in order to maintain their jobs.

As Beck states this involves a sense of individualisation, where the personal biographies become constituent elements of the workplace self. While *Nurse Jackie*'s biography is complex as it involves her identity as a prescription drug addict and adulterer, as much as a mother, a wife, a parent and a co-worker, the notion of female biography is central in the rise of "heroine television". For example within *Rhoda*, *Cagney and Lacey*, *NYPD Blue*, *Sex and The City*, a sense of female identity is played out through the main female characters' relationship to the workplace.

Rhoda and *Sex and the City* offer narratives that focus on leisure as much as work, where in the former the character of Rhoda Morgenstern (who originally appeared in *The Mary Tyler More Show* [1970–77]) is a native New Yorker who returns to the city (with her husband) setting up a window dressing company, and the latter focuses on a group of relatively wealthy female friends, whose professions include a popular culture journalist, art gallery manager, public relations manager and a lawyer. The narrative of these female characters focuses on their romantic and domestic lives as much as their professional workplace achievements and aspirations. Following the situation comedy format (see Chapter 2), a community narrative is presented that features New York as the setting for success in both leisure and work. It is this relationship to the city that is central in framing the feminist perspective.

For example, the opening sequence of *Rhoda* offers a personal resume of Rhoda's life so far. It opens with a direct-to-camera image of Rhoda as if presenting a video CV. She initially states, "My name is Rhoda Morgenstern. I was born in New York the Bronx in December 1941". Accompanied by family photos, and further accounts of her life including affirmation that she was a high school graduate, that she had moved to Minneapolis to work (referencing her character's appearance in *The Mary Tyler Moore Show*) and that she returned to Manhattan in New York, a sense of citizenship and ability to work in the city is presented. While some 20 years later the opening sequence of *Sex in the City* offers a similar diary like account of the lead character of Carrie Bradshaw. However instead of a voiceover, we are presented with a musical theme tune that evokes a Latin tango-like exoticism. The accompanying images are of Carrie Bradshaw set within the city, walking around as if in delight, pleasure and confidence, with intercut images of New York skyscrapers (such as the Chrysler building). The camera moves within the traffic, as if connoting that she is part of the throbbing heart of the city. Yet she is dressed in a party dress, which gets soaked with water as a bus passes by, leading Carrie to look back at the bus, not in anger but in pleasure as she reads an advert on the bus for her newspaper column, with the headline "Carrie Bradshaw Knows Good Sex". Both these opening sequences foreground the significance of New York, seeming like a place of opportunity and equality for females. While the characters in *Rhoda* and *Sex and The City* mostly focus on their interest in domesticity and the pursuit of satisfactory sexual and romantic life through framing the architecture and social world of New York, a sense of achievement and fulfilment is presented in living and working in the city.

The representation of New York, not only as a place of modernity and function, but also of cultural and ethnic diversity is central in our reading of "heroine television". For example as Liam Kennedy (2000) tells us:

> Confrontation with difference in urban space is a positional and rela-
> tional matter demarcating the self and the other, the citizen and the
> stranger and in some part dependent upon mental productions and cul-
> tural representations of stereotyping.
>
> (p. 7)

For example, the representation of women within the city as independent citizens offers a sense of strength and resolve, challenging the stereotype that women are subordinate to men. Women who can work and compete in the city place themselves within diverse social space, where they may be not only subject to stereotyping, but where they are also offered the opportunity to challenge those stereotypes of mother, wife, carer and homemaker. As part of this the city offers a space for identity reformation and challenge. As Kennedy (2000) suggests:

> Place, understood as a space of provisional self-definition or communal
> definition, remains powerfully effective in urban culture. Places are
> charged with emotional and mythical meanings; the location stories,
> images and memories associated with place can provide meaningful
> cultural and historical bearings for urban individuals and communities.
>
> (p. 7)

Characters represented within any particular place reference social and cultural divides that might be apparent in those places. While in *Maude*, *Rhoda* and *Sex and The City* social diversity might involve a focus on Jewish American identity, often as a context for humour, within *The Sopranos*, *Cagney and Lacey* and *NYPD Blue* there are more diverse social and cultural contexts, mapping the city as a relatively inhospitable environment.

As Kennedy (2000) tells us,

> New York and Los Angeles [alongside Chicago] may be considered as unevenly developed, polarised and segregated cities. With different degrees of critical consciousness and purpose they posit a paranoid urban imaginary which projects white fears and fantasies onto scenes of social disorder and degeneration.
>
> (p. 7)

For example in *Nurse Jackie*, the real-life setting of Saint Vincent's Hospital in Greenwich Village, the imagined inspiration for the fictional hospital of All Saints in the series (or at least its closure, see Chapter 5), offers a multicultural identity within New York itself. This setting not only intersects with issues of race and cosmopolitanism, but also as the first major hospital on the East Coast to have an HIV/AIDS centre (Boynton 2018), offers a focus on leading social care, prioritising social justice. Specifically the representation of nurses, who care for patients with HIV/AIDS, intersects with socio-economic and cultural aspects with regards to place and community. For example the work of nurse Helen Miramontes in HIV/AIDS activism was significant in this area, when at the height of the health crisis on a "national level . . . she organized and chaired a special task force on AIDS for the American Nurses Association" (USF 2018). Notably the representation of females working productively within healthcare and crime solving within the diverse cultural areas of New York offers a sense of strength and citizenship.

For example, while *Cagney and Lacey* and *NYPD Blue* are crime dramas, with the former focusing on two female police officers who work together, and the latter involving an ensemble cast which includes strong females in a similar manner to *St. Elsewhere* and *ER* (discussed above), despite this generic inconsistency, women are represented as efficient workers in crime solving and police work. As Jackie D'Acci (1987) advises considering *Cagney and Lacey*:

> The characters were represented as active subjects [who] were rarely represented as women in distress and virtually never rescued by their male colleagues, [with little reliance on] glamour at the levels of clothing, hairstyles and make up.
>
> (pp. 204–205)

Offering a landmark representation of women in the workplace, *Cagney and Lacey* may be considered as a feminist text that situates women as central heroic characters. However a central element within this is not so much their gender identity, but their relation to the work ethic, a central context within *Nurse Jackie*. As Beck and Beck-Gernsheim (2002) advise considering the last two decades of the twentieth century:

> As women were increasingly released from direct ties to the family, the female biography underwent an "individualisation boost" and, connected to this call, what functionalist theory calls a shift from "ascribed" to "acquired" roles.
>
> (p. 55)

For example, rather than performing the "ascribed" role of mother or wife or carer, the female characters take on self "acquired" roles such as nurses, lawyers and police officers, exhibiting the potential to compete within the workplace.

This is evident in the representation of the character of Diane Russell (played by Kim Delaney) in *NYPD Blue*. She is presented as a strong female police officer, with a complex and troubled life, yet she is as powerful as any male officer, if not more so. Although originally only a minor character in the series at the outset, from the third season she becomes a recurring character. We discover more of her life story, which involves her identity as a recovering alcoholic, who was abused by her father as a child, and who also had a miscarriage. Despite these signifiers of a troubled life, she is represented as an efficient and valued police officer. For example, consider a key sequence from season 8 of *NYPD Blue*. In a hostage situation, which is represented in an industrial building, a police officer named Manuel has been shot, and the police team communicate with the perpetrator called Denby via telephone observing his manic behaviour on surveillance cameras. Denby asks for Diane Russell to negotiate with him, as she is aware of his case having appeared to express concern and insight into his situation. After Diane enters the hostage room, and a relatively rational conversation takes place about the details of his crime, Denby becomes erratic, holding a gun to wounded officer Manuel's head.

Denby: I know that officer Manuel doesn't want to die today. . . . See he doesn't want to die. I do think someone is going to die today.
Diane: Don't do it Denby, or I'll have to shoot you.
Denby: Good because if you wanna' save him you'll have to.

Diane Russell immediately shots three shots into Denby, without hesitation, thereby saving the police officer and ending the hostage situation. While this representation might seem like a masculine performance, where a female character emulates what an efficient male officer might do, when we are aware of the life story of Diane Russell, we are aware that this is a performance that foregrounds her vulnerability, as much as her strength. In this sense her personal biography of vulnerability (as a victim of abuse, and an alcoholic) informs our reading of her strength in preforming the role of police officer.

Hence the representation of females in municipal roles such as within the police force or healthcare, in many instances challenge the hierarchy of masculine order through demonstrating an equality in workforce ability. Although in some instances females might be seen to emulate the imagined strength or intellectual insight allegedly held by male police officers and doctors in these roles, it is the audience's knowledge of the personal biography of the leading female protagonist as an element of "individualisation", that marks out this potential. As part of this the biography of the female, and the emotional universe of the character, may be considered as key elements of strength and resolve. This I argue extends from the representations of females in soap opera, as much as in crime drama, or hospital drama.

Soap Influences

Nurse Jackie presents an explicit connection to soap opera. This is not only evident in the titular name of the leading character of Jackie Peyton, which references the 1960s soap opera *Peyton Place* (1964–69), but also it is evident within the opening sequences of the pilot episode (discussed above) where Jackie Peyton seems to have overdosed and is lying on the hospital bathroom floor set within a 1960s mise en scène, including institutional dress and environment, typical of the nursing profession at that time. At the same time the 1960s family and the domestic iconography is fantasised in the closing episode of the first season, where this image reappears, however this time she actually does overdose. As she lies on the floor she casually looks to her side, where we see a morphed saturated colour image of her family with husband Kevin in the company of her two young children dressed in 1960s middle-class clothing in an idealistic bungalow garden. They appear to be waving at her in a gleeful stance, connoting an idealistic soap opera scene.

Hence from the outset in season 1 bookending the first and last episode, *Nurse Jackie* is coded as a nostalgic soap opera. This reference is significant, as while many hospital dramas could be considered as soap operas as much as medical procedural dramas (such as body trauma TV, discussed earlier), it is the tension between these two forms that is central.

Significantly, not only does *Nurse Jackie* reference the notion of nostalgic soap opera, but also I would argue that this is a recurring motif within many exemplars of "body trauma TV". For example, within *House* (also discussed above) the lead character of Gregory House steals time away from his work in medical diagnosis to find pleasure in watching the soap opera drama *General Hospital* (1963–), where he is represented as commenting on the romantic and domestic narratives of the series. Added to this it is important to note that many medical dramas may be considered as soap operas in terms of form besides *General Hospital*, such as *Casualty* (1986–) and *Holby City* (1999–) which have consistently been broadcast in the manner of soap operas framing a recurring domestic relationship with their audiences.

While soap opera could be considered as a lesser form than medical drama (or body trauma TV), in its focus on the everyday domestic community, rather than a focus on the energy of medical practice in working on diagnoses and healing, I argue that it is the soap opera-like nature of *Nurse Jackie* that actually offers depth for diverse audiences. Specifically, this may be apparent in how the series situates female characters. As Christine Geraghty (1991) informs us considering the constitution of soap opera for audiences, "Enjoyment will be affected by the way in which the woman viewer is herself positioned within the home as mother/wife/daughter" (p. 40). Furthermore "consistent recognition is given to the emotional situations which women are deemed to share" (p. 47). Hence a sense of sharing is provided within the representations, foregrounding similarities in emotional and cultural experience, such as references to family, community and romantic relationships.

However as Seiter et al. (1989) have discussed with regards for the potential for female audiences to "read" soap operas, based on research done in Oregon:

> Class, among many other factors, plays a major role in how our respondents make sense of the text. The experience of working-class women clearly conflicts in substantial ways with the soap opera's representation of women's problems, problems some identified as upper or middle class.
>
> (p. 241)

Although notions of female experience may be seen to be universal, such as being a mother, or a sister, or potentially running a household, issues of class may be pivotal in how audiences may engage or disengage with the text. For example, lower class female audiences might not necessarily engage with representations of upper of middle class women. This might certainly be evident in considering the soap opera-like narratives of *Dallas* (1978–91) and *Dynasty* (1981–89), where we are presented with the life stories of the super-rich, and lower class audiences could view the lives that are presented here as exotic, and disconnected from their own experiences.

Despite this, Ien Ang (2007) has defined the concept of "emotional realism", in assessing the responses of viewers of *Dallas*:

> Most female fans loved the show through identification with its melodramatic imagination, that is, by adopting a viewing position that affirms the emotional realism of a "tragic structure of feeling" represented by the soap opera: these viewers enjoyed being swept away by the heightened, if not exaggerated, emotional highs and lows of the narrative.
>
> (p. 21)

Hence a sense of intense identification might be related to an overemphasis on emotions, substance or style. Added to this it is possible to argue that some audiences might engage with a television programme not so much as they "realistically" identify, or emphasise with the narrative or the character, but irony may play a part in the viewing pleasure. For example, Ang (2007) advises that:

> This affective mode of pleasure, which is based on taking melodrama seriously, can be contrasted by a very different mode of enjoyment; what I called ironic pleasure. This is a mode of viewing that is informed by a more intellectually distancing, superior subject position which could afford having pleasure in the show while simultaneously expressing a confident knowingness about its supposedly "low" quality.
>
> (p. 21)

Whilst it is impossible to assess the "true" nature of audience identification, these viewing positions are significant, in reading soap opera. Particularly for *Nurse Jackie*, which might be seen to offer intellectual critical insight in the representation of a drug addict who is proficient at healthcare, elements of irony may be apparent. This may be relevant not so much in assessing the "low" quality of the narrative or the form, but may be apparent within the sophisticated narrative representations.

For example, if we consider the initial episodes of *Nurse Jackie* in comparison to early narratives in *ER*, with particular regard to female representation within the workplace, diverse and relatively sophisticated contexts of engagement may be apparent.

Nurse Jackie almost exclusively focuses on the character of Jackie Peyton. As discussed above from the outset of the series, we are given access to her moral universe, framing her personal dilemmas in relation to her addiction to prescription drugs and her ability to do her job. The narrative concerns a central focus on her efficiency in doing her job, and her professional and domestic value within the workplace, and at home. In the opening episode, not only does she frequently take drugs while also nourishing an adulterous relationship with the hospital department pharmacist Eddie, who essentially is her drug dealer, but also she cares for patients, and is seen to be a valued colleague at work, and a caring mother at home. The audience are presented with her conflicted moral universe, in her representation at work and at home.

In contrast *ER* has no central character, and rather features an ensemble cast that are given an equal focus at different times, depending on the narrative arc of each episode. Consisting of six central characters in the first season, whilst four are male and only two are female, it is significant that the male characters are largely resident doctors/surgeons or intern doctors, while only one of the female characters is a doctor, and the other is a nurse, Carol Hathaway. Whilst Carol might appear as a subordinate character, she is represented as a central narrative context over the first three episodes, within season 1. This narrative however does not focus on her ability as a nurse in the manner of *Nurse Jackie*; rather it concerns her vulnerability after she attempts suicide, in the pilot episode.

While Jackie Peyton in *Nurse Jackie* and Carol Hathaway (played by Juliana Marguiles) in *ER* seem entirely different characters in terms of workplace identity, they are both the central figures that bond the narrative, albeit in entirely different ways. Although Carol may seem peripheral compared to Jackie (evident in her proficiency in doing her job), while Carol seems like a support nurse, both characters represent the emotional universe of the workplace. In the case of Jackie, this may be evident in her robust and confident interaction with work colleagues. For example, this is apparent where Jackie admonishes Coop for failing to detect a bleed in a patient that dies because of this (in the pilot episode), where she performs the Heimlich manoeuvre on a stranger at a restaurant in the presence of a colleague while just having lunch (pilot episode), and where she treats a disturbed man and offers him creative social care advice even though he had violently punched her in the face just a few hours earlier (Season 1, Ep. 2). She is represented as professional, confident and articulate in the role, seeming like a pivotal member of the workplace team.

Although the representation of Carol within *ER* seems far less dynamic, she similarly is represented as a valued unit in the workplace. For example, when in episode one at the close of the narrative the team learn of her suicide attempt, practically the entire workforce come to her support and resuscitate her, and all gather around in the nature that members of an army look after "one of their own". When she returns to work some eight weeks later (in episode 3) after receiving psychiatric support, rather than her being viewed as an "other" and somehow damaged and potentially unrepairable, she is almost irreverently reminded that she is part of the team, and not an outsider.

This takes initial form as a ruse. After being told that Mark is hurt, she rushes into a crowded room, to the rousing welcome of "surprise!", and applause from those secretly gathered there. Colleague Mark Green then makes a speech, advising that she had "managed to grab our attention", offering a light-hearted tone. She is given a novelty hat to wear seemingly made of surgical supplies, which has the words "welcome back" hand written on it, in the manner of a scrawl. She smiles and puts the hat on, then stands on the chair to make a speech to the assembled crowd there, in the manner of the best man's speech at a wedding. She tells them: "To say I feel lucky would be kind of an understatement. What you all did to save me was like a gift, I promise to remember that every day, so thank you". Rather than treating her differently, with individuals asking reasons why she attempted suicide, she is treated to a carnivalesque display of revelry. This sense of inclusivity and playfulness, not only highlights her position as a valued member of the team, but also stimulates the audience to engage with the text in productive ways.

The characters of Jackie Peyton in *Nurse Jackie* and Carol Hathaway in *ER* offer an almost ironic prospect in viewing their contribution to the workplace environment. While Jackie's team are not fully aware of her drug taking at this stage, and Carol's colleagues probably cannot imagine what it is like to have gone through a suicide attempt, the audience are provided with a viewing position that is unresolved, and ambiguous. It is this viewing position where nothing is explicit between the characters, yet the audience witness a sense of close union and partnership that may seem tentative or ephemeral, which provides a "structure of feeling" for the audience to engage with. Our identification with these characters, as providing an ambiguous emotional narrative space, is made stronger through the ironic juxtaposition of "internal" and "external" monologues. Jackie and Carol are not easily understood, but the representation of a drug addict that can perform well within the healthcare industry, and the representation of a person that is recovering from a suicide attempt could be greeted with humour, breaks down barriers of moral judgement, or abject signification. We cannot really know what it is like to have experienced these events (unless we have done them ourselves), but we are provided with an ambiguous vision that resists a melodramatic saturated sense of emotion by making everything known, in the manner of soap opera. These female representations encourage a sense of thinking through whilst suspending judgement, and the notion of fixed ideals.

Conclusion

Nurse Jackie is a complex text. An exemplar of body trauma TV and heroine television, with contextual references to soap opera and to some degree situation comedy (see Chapter 2), a hybridised narrative vision is presented that largely focuses on the significance of female identity within the work-place. While some may argue that Jackie Peyton is an unfit role model of a healthcare professional, evident in her relationship to drug addiction, and her contemptuous respect for practice regulation and management hierarchy (see Nemeth 2011), she inevitably offers a vivid site for identification and/or disdain.

While I have discussed a range of diverse fictional media texts that could be foundational or contextual, such as *Maude, The Sopranos, Rhoda, Sex and the City, House* and *ER*, where similarly female identity is related to the workplace and the usefulness of labour, central within this is the notion of "emotional realism". While Ien Ang (2007) suggests that often this involves a "tragic structure of feeling" with "viewers enjoy[ing] being 'swept away' by the heightened, if not exaggerated, emotional highs and lows of the narrative" (p. 21), this sense of exaggeration is significant in our reading of *Nurse Jackie*.

Through the viewer being offered an insight into the trials and tribulations of a healthcare professional that is addicted to prescription drugs, while judgement may inevitably encourage a reading that assigns culpability, equally the viewer must assess professional ability, even if in the representation it is achieved through dubious or improper means. This may lead the viewer to consider that "the end justifies the means"—if a life is saved, and the emotional journey of that rescue, allows you to suspend rules regards proper practice and social interaction, then this offers a meaningful sense of "emotional realism".

Despite this we could equally argue that *Nurse Jackie* is not exclusively a cypher for female identity, and in effect represents something far wider and more encompassing. As we shall see in the following chapter, *Nurse Jackie* potentially offers a meaningful critique on the American Dream, where drug addiction might not exclusively be related to workplace identity, but rather interrogates deeper cultural issues of inequality, disavowal and disrepair.

Note

1. All Saints Hospital is actually set in Baruch College, New York, Newman Vertical Campus (see Baruch 2018).

2 The American Dream and the Absent Mother

Introduction

In the pilot episode of *Nurse Jackie* (2009–15), the titular character of Jackie Peyton consoles the girlfriend of a young man who only a few hours before had passed away from a head trauma resulting in a bleed to the brain (see also Chapter 1). Only just arriving at the hospital, the girlfriend recalls how earlier in that same day, it had seemed like any other day, affirming her ideal life together with the victim: "he made pancakes this morning". Later at the end of the episode, when Jackie returns home from a hard day at work, her children are playing in the living room, and her husband is busy in the kitchen. To raise her spirits, he greets her with: "I made pancakes! How good is that!" The significance of this idealised representation of domesticity is central in our reading of *Nurse Jackie*, as when Jackie hears these words, there is an irony in its meaning, juxtaposing the earlier instance which represents ideal love and loss. Jackie may not be worthy of a loving partner "making her pancakes", as she has a secret adulterous relationship with Eddie the hospital pharmacist (who is the supplier of her drugs), and her workplace colleagues are largely unaware that she has a family, let alone a husband, involving a ritual she makes every morning on arriving at work where she conceals her wedding band. *Nurse Jackie* represents a critique of idealised domesticity, framing the notion of the "absent mother" (Harwood 1997, p. 104) or ideal partner, as a failure of the American Dream.

This chapter consequently considers *Nurse Jackie* in relation to the American dream, framing aspects of irony and critique. As part quality television and situation comedy (besides as an exemplar of medical drama, heroine television and soap opera—see Chapter 1), *Nurse Jackie* foregrounds the American Dream as a central point of reference, framing the notion of the mother or the ideal partner, or wife. In the manner that the making of pancakes represents the ideal domestic American breakfast (or supper) for a loving and productive couple living the dream life, the pilot episode sets the tone for the series, framing imagined pleasure and fulfilment as coexistent with issues of loss, deception and irony. At the same time part of this involves a focus on her addiction to prescription drugs, and her relationship to an opiate addiction epidemic in the United States (Quinones 2016). I argue that the interrelationship of the American Dream and opiate addiction of many US citizens forms an essential narrative cultural element in defining the meaning of the series.

Situation Comedy and Quality Television

The concept of the American dream is central within both American situation comedy and the notion of "quality television". For example Gerald Jones in *Honey, I'm Home!: Sitcoms: Selling The American Dream* (1993) directly relates the significance of family and domesticity in the narratives of situation comedy, exploring key early texts such as *I Love Lucy* (1951–57), *All in the Family* (1971–79) and *The Simpsons* (1989–). At the same time "quality television", is a term that has become synonymous with high quality television programmes (from the later 1990s) often made by subscription television channels such as HBO, extending from the emergence of shows like *The Sopranos* (see Ricci 2014; Yacowar 2007). Quality television may be considered as "must see TV" (see McCabe and Akass 2007), offering a direct resonance not only to high quality production values and "quality" scripts, but also to a wider sense of shared community and/or cultural heritage, evident in the concept of the American Dream. For example, besides *The Sopranos* in which Edie Falco who plays Jackie Peyton in *Nurse Jackie* also starred within playing the lead character of Carmela Soprano (the wife of a Mafia boss), landmarks shows include *Six Feet Under* (2001–05), *The Wire* (2002–08) and *Breaking Bad* (2008–13). These shows offer a critique of the American Dream, in their focus on mortality and the meaning of the American Family, at the same time contextualising sexuality, minority identity, drug use and consumerism.

These shows, like many others that may be considered as "quality television" represent American life, possibly offering deep social commentary, critical of "new beginnings" (Gabrielson 2009). Hence both situation comedy and quality television offer direct references to the notion not only of domesticity and family, but also that of aspiration and achievement within society, evident in the concept of the American Dream.

Whilst early situation comedies such as *I Love Lucy* and *All in the Family* might offer relatively earnest representations of the American Dream, with an ideal domesticity presented in the former, and a critique of achieving the dream in the latter, it is this focus on the dream as contextual to family life in the definition of aspirations, goals and possible reward that is central. In

I Love Lucy, when Desi Arnaz (as Ricky Ricardo) announces "Lucy, I'm home" to wife Lucille Ball (as Lucy Ricardo) both in semi-autobiographical fictional roles where a real life couple seemed to appear as themselves, a reference is made to the archetypal American Family where a Cuban American immigrant breadwinner returns to an ideal family home. Also while in *All in the Family* (an adaptation of the UK show *Till Death Us Do Part*) there is more of a focus on social commentary and a shift to realism, where implications of race, sexuality and gender were more significantly explored within the concept of family, a central concern remains the function of the everyday family life.

Situation comedy and quality television are inherent elements within *Nurse Jackie*. With regard to situation comedy, not only is this is evident in the series in relation to the focus on the family, and the American dream, but it is also evident with regards to the structural form of the programme itself. *Nurse Jackie* complies with the usual structural rules of situation comedy; that a programme is usually of 30 minutes duration (including adverts, if there are any), it is focused on a community or group of friends within a particular setting, that it references cultural and social stereotypes, and that there is a circular narrative (see Bowes 1990). While in the latter it is possible to argue that *Nurse Jackie* breaks this rule as it presents the meta narrative of addiction, evident in Jackie's long-term narrative journey, in fact largely in structural terms each episode returns to a particular narrative point, referencing its circular resolution. For example, in many episodes of *Nurse Jackie*, Jackie Peyton is represented as at home at the start of the episode, and returns to home by the close of the episode, often reflecting on a working day. Although following a convention that appears in later situation comedies such as *Friends* (1994–2004), where it seems that the narrative progresses as the life stories of the characters change (such as the progress of Jackie Peyton's addiction, Doctor O'Hara becomes pregnant, junior nurse Zoey's career progresses, as does her love life), structurally *Nurse Jackie* employs the regular conventions of situation comedy.

Nurse Jackie also complies with the formal expectations of situation comedy, with regards to community setting and stereotyping. Like its predecessor in medical drama *Scrubs* (2001–10), the setting of a hospital and the representation of a workplace team is not that unusual. Comedic elements are largely mediated in our knowledge of cultural stereotypes. In *Scrubs* this involves the narratives of new interns working in healthcare, and the friendship bonds that may be formed, relative to inexperience and youth. In *Nurse Jackie* stereotypes surround the roles of nurses and doctors, with a particular focus on challenging the stereotypes that doctors diagnose, while nurses heal. We know not only that Jackie Peyton challenges the authority of doctors to diagnose, but also that as a drug addict herself, she may be stereotyped as a patient rather than as a healer. In this sense irony is present in that she has great ability to do her job as a nurse, but as she is "diseased", she seems more like a patient, as someone needing care.

Despite *Nurse Jackie*'s generic code as situation comedy, it is important to note that it represents a hybrid form in the manner that later situation comedies involved irony or playfulness, such as within *Scrubs*. Unlike earlier situation comedy, which might have more earnestly represented ideal family life in *I Love Lucy* and *All in the Family*, *Nurse Jackie* presents a sense of playfulness in representing family life and the American Dream.

A challenge to the meta narrative of the American Dream may be evident in the concept of postmodernity. As Anthony Elliott (1996) tells us:

> The [modern] grand narratives that unified and structured Western science and philosophy, grounding truth and meaning in the presumption of a universal subject and a predetermined goal of emancipation, no longer appear convincing or even plausible. . . . [Postmodern] [k]nowledge is constructed, not discovered; it is contextual, not foundational.
>
> (p. 19)

Such contextual appropriation of knowledge or representation within contemporary situation comedies, such as *Scrubs* and *Nurse Jackie*, break down hierarchies of form and identity. Specifically if we consider the notion of the American Dream, and its relationship to new beginnings, or wish fulfilment, evident in the achievement of a secure emotional life world also involving financial security, *Nurse Jackie* offers a postmodern critique of these ideals.

For example if we consider the pilot episode, this not only includes the narrative of the deceased bike messenger, whose girlfriend states that earlier in the day "he made pancakes" (as discussed above), but also another young girl is brought to the emergency room having been subject to a knife attack. We discover that this girl is a prostitute, and during the attack she managed to defend herself with a knife, cutting off the ear of her assailant, who we find out later is her client for sexual services, and also a diplomat. The juxtaposition between these two vulnerable young women—one who has lost her boyfriend and who seems to have had an ideal romantic partnership, and the other who has to sell her body to make a living, but becomes a victim of attack—frames the narratives of ideal family/romance in contrast with sex work to make a living. *Nurse Jackie* parodies the notion of the American Dream under these themes, through representing the punishment of those that might stop you achieving the dream life that you have "paid for", and through redistributing wealth as a means to achieve your dream life.

This is apparent when, after the prostitute's assailant is brought to the emergency room, rather than ensuring that his severed ear is medically preserved so it may be reattached through an operation, Jackie Peyton disposes of it. After Jackie discovers that the assailant not only has immunity as a diplomat and consequently will not pay for his attack on the prostitute, but also that he is unrepentant, she swiftly takes the ear to the bathroom, holds the ear up to her face, says "fuck you", then flushes it down a water closet. Besides this, as further retribution, she takes money from the wallet of the diplomat when he is not looking, and surreptitiously passes on the money to the girlfriend of the deceased bike messenger, though slipping it into her belongings. Through punishing the unrepentant diplomat, and redistributing his wealth, all the while defending the prostitute, she parodies the constituent elements of the American Dream.

Within *Nurse Jackie* the meta narratives of striving for financial and emotional security inherent in the American Dream are "decentred and dispersed" (Elliott 1996, p. 19) through a postmodern focus on surface and collage (see Jameson 1991; Woods 1999), where Jackie Peyton redistributes wealth, and ensures that crimes are paid for, rather than the state offering the means to make this happen. *Nurse Jackie* does not however present an explicit message, but rather it frames the contexts of engagements, and the potential for individuals to intervene.

American Dream and Opiate Addiction

Nurse Jackie's relationship to situation comedy, and that of quality TV are central in its mediation and critique of the American Dream. As Teena Gabrielson (2009) advises with regards to quality television and the American Dream within shows such as *The Sopranos*, *Weeds* and *Lost*, "the concept of a new beginning is tied to a resource rich, but uncultivated, landscape that offers the materials by which the individual might attain both economic security and domestic felicity". For the drug addict, however, the American Dream seems unattainable, as economic and domestic life are disturbed, and a sense of ending, rather than beginning, pervades. As Sam Quinones informs us in the preface to his landmark book *Dreamland: The True Tale of America's Opiate Addiction* (2016), framing the historical significance of a swimming pool named Dreamland in Portsmouth, Ohio, USA, as an idealised place representing the American Dream that could be lost through the advance of opiate addiction:

> All of this recreation let a working class family feel well off. But the centre of it all was that gleaming, glorious swimming pool. Memories of Dreamland, drenched in the smell of chlorine, Coppertone and French fries, were what almost everyone who grew up in Portsmouth took with them as the town declined. Two Portsmouths exist today. One

is a town of abandoned buildings at the edge of the Ohio River. The other resides in the memories of thousands in the town's diaspora who grew up during its better years and returned to the actual Portsmouth rarely if at all. When you ask them what the time was back then, it was Dreamland.

(p. 4)

Framing the medium of the swimming pool as a social space of connectivity and pleasure, at the same time referencing the consumer products that may be purchased and consumed there, a socio-historical account is presented that frames issues of loss.

However, the loss of the American dream is attributed to those that can no longer function as ideal citizens now weighed down by opiate addiction, as their aspirations and life chances evaporate. The metaphor of the swimming pool is significant, as it represents an idealised meeting place where multiple communities converge, offering a sense of democracy through playfulness and shared leisure activity. Yet this community seems to be lost, and the pool represents an empty space, rather than a meeting point. This sense of absence is related to a loss of an immersive carefree idealised "dreamland" of meeting, exchange and equality, and rather a new immersion in drugs as a divergent "dreamland" in taking away your identity.

Sam Quinones tells the story of the advance of opiate addiction and the shift to a divergent dreamland, framing key moments in the development of painkillers, particularly highlighting the introduction of OxyContin in the USA back in 1996, and the significance of the manufacturers, Perdue.

OxyContin [took the properties and extended] an earlier Perdue product: MS Contin. MS Contin was Perdue's first foray into pain management using the Continus time release formula invented by Napp in England. MS Contin sent morphine into a patient's bloodstream continuously—hence Contin—over several hours. . . . In preparing OxyContin for sale, Perdue thought it was just an extension of MS Contin.

(pp. 124–125)

Hence the development of OxyContin was an idealistic one, where a drug's time-release property that would enable a continuous release of painkillers into the bloodstream would be seen as a desirable property, seeming to meet increasing demands in pain management. However the manufacturers of OxyContin had not believed that the drug would be addictive, as prior drugs that they had developed involving time-release properties such as MS Contin weren't found to be so addictive. The president of Perdue at that time, Win Gerson, is quoted as stating: "There was nothing that suggested in reading the data that five minutes after you marketed it the kids would learn how to break it down" (cited in Quinones 2016, p. 125).

However, the key element was not so much the time-release property, it was the marketing of the drug itself. MS Contin was marketed to cancer patients and people just out of surgery, either for those at the end of their lives, or those needing short-term pain management, while OxyContin was marketed more generally. Quinones tells us:

> The company aimed to convince doctors to aggressively treat noncancer pain, and prescribe OxyContin for moderate pain lasting more than a few days. OxyContin ought to be used for bad backs, knee pain tooth extraction, headaches, fibromyalgia, as well as football, hockey and dirt bike injuries, broken bones, and, of course, after surgery. This was a vast new market for an opiate painkiller.
>
> (p. 127)

As the market was widened for what was an opiate drug that could be easily transformed into "hard core drugs" through crushing, this presented new forms of access and engagement. General users who may have experienced for example long-term back pain gain access to opiate drugs that might be addictive (whether they were crushed or not), potentially leads to a reliance on street drugs (such as heroin) when the prescription runs out. Also the drug itself as able to be transformed through crushing would be appealing to those already addicted to opiates.

A focus on opiate addiction may be seen as a central element in key texts within quality television. For example in both *The Wire* and *Breaking Bad*, the latter of which is titled as a reference to dangers of "breaking down" opiate drugs, drug addiction in relation to supply and demand are key narrative elements in framing the loss of the American Dream. In *Breaking Bad* the central character is diagnosed with cancer, and the only way he can survive to pay for treatment is to utilise his professional skills in chemistry to produce hard core drugs such as Crystal Meth, and sell to the vulnerable. In *The Wire* an impoverished community is held ransom to a drug addiction culture that is embedded as the only means to survive, in continuing the abject cycle of supply and demand. Central within this is a focus on the advance of opiate addiction within the mainstream, and the ease of which individuals become addicted, largely made possible through the greed of pharmaceutical companies failing to predict drug misuse and "breaking down".

Although *Nurse Jackie* does not explicitly tell the story of OxyContin as discussed above, it relentlessly replicates the process of mis-using drugs by breaking them down. Continuously throughout *Nurse Jackie*, from the opening moments of the pilot episode to the final episode some seven seasons later, Jackie Peyton crushes drugs (or opens up capsules) like OxyContin or Percocet to get her immediate fix, often through "snorting" the drug. Within the series the character of Jackie Peyton states the dangers of this, in an ironic statement as if reading the warning notice on the drugs container:

> *Percocet should never be crushed, broken or chewed*: unless you want it to hit your blood stream like a bolt of lightning.
>
> (Season 1, Ep. 2)

However, while *Nurse Jackie* does not tell the story of how the conditions arrived for the abuse of opiate drugs, which were made more easily available through changes in marketing, it reveals the effects of such use, in framing the loss of the American Dream.

If we consider the fourth season of *Nurse Jackie*, this may be considered as the pivotal season, suggesting a turning point, and a sense of coming to terms is apparent, where Jackie Peyton admits herself to rehab. At the end of season 3 Jackie's life is falling apart, when her husband discovers that she is addicted to drugs and admits having an affair, and as a kind of revenge her lover Eddie the ER pharmacist had made friends with Jackie's husband. Also despite a period of trying to get off drugs with the support of friends, she is using again. Also at the start of season 4 we discover that All Saints Hospital has been sold to a private conglomerate, and there are changes in management. Besides this, Jackie's husband Kevin petitions for divorce, after discovering that she had been having an affair with Eddie, and Kevin severely beats him up.

Jackie is represented as hitting a new low in the opening episode of season 4, where she picks up a young drug addict when she visits a church while lighting a candle at the altar, when their hands accidentally touch. After taking the man back to her home for a drug-taking binge, now empty as her husband has moved out (and her children are away with him), the young man has a heart attack and dies. In a carnivalesque sequence where she gets her best friend Dr O'Hara to sign an illegal death certificate, and arranges for colleague Zoey and her ambulance driver boyfriend to take the body away, she decides that she has reached a new low, and books herself into rehab.

Although keen to get through rehab as quick as possible, only staying 16 days when she should have remained for a month, it is during this time that we learn of the origins of her drug taking and its relationship to her family, and by token the American Dream. Rather than following the stereotype of those that might have become addicted to prescription drugs such as prescription opiates (discussed above) that might happen through treatment for pain, *Nurse Jackie* eventually admits that her addiction is connected to her daughter Grace. Jackie tells the rehab group that she felt that her child didn't identify with her, and after a little time she turned to opiates that she had access to in hospital to make her feel better. Hence inverting the narrative of availability and treatment for physical pain, Jackie's addiction stems from her imagined failure to be a good mother, related to psychological stress at home.

The Absent and Unstable Mother

However as Jim Cullen (2003) considers the "overlooked costs of dreaming" (p. 7), achieving the role of the ideal mother within the context of the American family inevitably is problematic. As Cullen attests: "Ambiguity is the very source of its mystic power, nowhere more so than among those striving for, but unsure whether they will reach, their goals" (p. 7). The achievement of the American dream, in forming the ideal family that might be well catered for, and able to progress in the world, offers up problems for individuals to solve, as achievement is subjective and contextual.

Nurse Jackie mediates these ideas, through presenting Jackie as an exemplar of the nurturing and caring mother archetypes (Jung 2002). As Edie Falco herself in a documentary trailer on the series tells us in identifying the meaning of her character:

> A nurse is kind of the ultimate mother job. It's not just the technicalities of putting gauze on wounds, taking temperatures and IVs, and all that stuff. There is a soulful, spiritual connection that they need to have with the patients as well.
>
> (YouTube 2018f)

As part of this not only is she caring and motherly at work in the hospital, but also we see this potential with reference to her relation to colleagues and friends.

However as Peggy Phelan (1993) points out concerning the representation of pregnancy, the mother is an unstable representational figure:

> The (Symbolic) Mother will never be their "proper" subject of psychoanalysis and will always be a problematic subject for Western art because as an image who potentially contains the other within one continuous body, she reeks havoc with the notion of symmetry and reciprocity fundamental to understanding the exchange of gaze operative in both.
>
> (p. 30)

This problematic interrelation between the spectator and the mother, finding the maternal figure as a challenge to the representational order, is explicitly framed within *Nurse Jackie*. Specifically in season 4 (Ep. 4) what appears to be a drunken irresponsible pregnant woman is admitted to hospital. However, later it is revealed that she has a rare form of untreatable cancer, which enlarges her abdomen giving the appearance of pregnancy. At the same time in season 5 (Ep. 5), a heavily pregnant women is urgently brought to hospital has just been shot, and the team swiftly deliver the baby whilst she is splayed on the entrance floor of the emergency department. In both of these instances, issues of instability and misrecognition are framed with regard to the representation of the pregnant mother, manifest in relation to mortality as having cancer, or being shot. As an unstable figure, the mother (pregnant or otherwise) offers a complex representational prospect. This involves not only an intimation of instability, or disorder, but also forms references to culpability, in terms of interaction with the physical world.

As a number of feminist theorists have argued with regards to the representation of mothers within the media (Kaplan 1992; Modeleski 1991), a hegemonic semiotic system exists within popular culture that associates the good mother with passivity, evident in the need to be compliant or stay at home, and the bad mother with activity, evident in the troubling pursuit of a personal or professional life outside the domestic world. Hence a mother that pursues a career outside home, potentially competing with men in a professional, or wider cultural world, inevitably will be coded as failing to meet the standards required of the ideal mother.

While Jackie Peyton is represented as an exemplar of a mother, evident in her caring ability at work in the hospital, she is signified as an absent or failing mother at home. Significantly, Jackie's attraction to drugs is intrinsically linked to her imagined failure to be a good mother, in her inability to cope with Grace as a child. She became an "active mother", evident in her pursuit of drugs as a means to cope with the psychological rejection that she believed that she received from her child. She is also active, in her dedication to her professional work, while separating her family life from this world. This is particularly evident in Jackie Peyton's long-term concealment of her domestic life from the majority of her peers.

The representation of the ideal mother as passive, and the problematic mother as active, engages with the wider notion of presence and absence. If a mother is represented as fully participating within the domestic sphere, staying at home, caring for the children, she potentially may be rewarded through conforming to the stereotypical archetype of the nurturing and caring mother. However, if the mother is represented as absent, potentially spending too much time outside the domestic space, possibly taking on a professional role, or seemingly indulging herself in the pursuit of leisure, inattentive to the needs of the family, theoretically she may be coded as needing punishment.

As Sarah Harwood (1997) in examining the representations of family in 1980s Hollywood film, tells us:

> The family organises, and gives meaning to, a multiple complex of discursive formations. Family discourses structures our understanding of how society reproduces and manages itself and how individuals are inserted into it.
>
> (p. 37)

Hence notions such as the American Dream, are reliant on the discursive constitution of the family, relating individuals' interrelationship to each other within the family unit. At the head of this archetypal and stereotypical form of family are the mother and father, but there is an over-reliance on the father, as he is coded in society as the breadwinner, or the leader of the family unit. However, as Harwood affirms:

> Whereas the father attempts to fix the family through establishing his own inherently unstable role [evident in the need to lead and direct, possibly taking risks in service of providing security], mothers have an inherent representational stability and render the family unstable by any deviation from an ideological norm.
>
> (p. 102)

As such if the mother is absent from the home environment, in a manner that the father may be, this represents a deviation from the normative structures that provide psychological and social security. Consequently, "[a]s the mother is intrinsically defined by the family it is perhaps a tautology to point out that her absence destroys it" (p. 104).

While the representation of Jackie Peyton offers insight into her maternal nurturing ability, largely this is represented as outside the domestic environment, and hence she may be coded as an absent mother. However, as the family unit offers the means to frame meaningful narratives of identity, community and achievement, such as evident in the American Dream, Jackie Peyton is a displaced or unresolved absent mother, inevitably needing to respond, or compensate for her situation as outside.

Sarah Harwood (1997) in defining the narrative potential of the absent mother tells us, framing her case study of 1980s Hollywood films, citing exemplars such as *Indiana Jones and The Last Crusade* (1989), *Pretty Woman* (1990) and *Rain Man* (1989), that when mothers are absent:

> [These] films rehearse three distinct but complimentary narrational responses to the mother's absence. In the first child is unable to achieve

maturation. . . . The second response marks the collapse of intra family terms, in which the child also becomes the father or vice versa and the mother's procreative function is usurped. . . . The third response is to privilege the extra domestic, the metaphorical family.

(p. 104)

In many ways this typology based on findings in film is applicable to the representation of Jackie Peyton as an absent mother. For example, the absence of Jackie Peyton seems to contribute to her daughter Grace's psychological problems, which seem to involve a lack of maturity, evident where she seems disturbed, in the manner that a child might grow up that has been neglected. The family seems to collapse, where Jackie's husband Kevin becomes childlike, evident in his pursuit of a punitive divorce arrangement that lacks an adult or mature approach. Significantly, Jackie forms an extra domestic metaphorical family with work colleagues, which in many ways appears as a substitute family. Hence these representations present the punitive measures assigned to absent mothers who may seem to neglect the procreative family.

Despite this, it is possible to argue that these narrative responses to the threat of the absent mother, in fact offer a deeper level of engagement that reflects the complexity of motherhood in relation to the struggle of addiction. For example, if we consider her relationship with her extra domestic metaphorical family, Jackie in many ways is coded as a child, as much as the mother, offering a sense of need rather than punishment. For example if we consider the relationship she has between Dr Eleanor O'Hara (played by Eve Best), her best friend in the first five seasons, and her relationship with rehab sponsor Antoinette White (played by Julie White) in season 6, these relationships may be considered as pivotal in terms of support to Jackie outside or beyond the workplace. Jackie's relationship with Dr O'Hara offers a complex journey of support, where in the initial season O'Hara is the only workplace colleague that is aware that she is married and has a family, and they consistently have lunch together, with O'Hara taking Jackie to expensive restaurants. Later O'Hara not only offers financial support to Jackie, to allow Grace to attend a better school (where it is thought that her psychological state might improve), but also O'Hara does her best to help Jackie get off drugs, offering financial support for rehab, and involving herself in illegal practice to conceal Jackie's identity as a drug addict. This is evident where O'Hara offers to informally prescribe drugs to alleviate Jackie's addiction, plus she helps Jackie conceal the death of a drug addict at Jackie's home, by providing a death certificate (discussed above). Similarly in season 6, Antoinette takes on the role of confidant and supporter to Jackie, in many ways replacing Dr O'Hara. While their connection is made through rehab, rather than the workplace, Antoinette offers deep psychological support to Jackie. For example not long after they first meet at an AA meeting, and initially Jackie is uncertain of her, advising that she is not good with authority, Antoinette consoles Jackie: "I am very good with people who are not good with authority, I am not so good as a role model". From this point Antoinette becomes Jackie's rehab sponsor. At the same time in some ways she is a role model, as she has been sober for ten years, but is willing to intimate to Jackie the trial of relapse, indicating a number of times that she has done this herself. Both Dr O'Hara and Antoinette present themselves as parent-like figures to Jackie, who offer support beyond the means of regular friends.

However, Jackie's relationship with O'Hara and Antoinette, respectively, ultimately frames issues of vulnerability and imbalance, as much as mutual and equal respect. For example when at the start of season 5 O'Hara returns from pregnancy leave, she makes an impromptu decision to return to the United Kingdom. This occurs at a point when Jackie is particularly vulnerable through her husband attempting to gain custody of her children, and an awkward exchange occurs between Jackie and O'Hara, where Jackie questions O'Hara's motives in leaving the hospital to take care of her child.

O'Hara: When you were on probation, spending all that time with your kids.

Jackie: It was great, and then I came back to work [Getting agitated], because that is what we do. There are all kinds of people here who depend on you.

O'Hara: Actually one person depends on me, and I have to be there for him. I don't want my child growing up hating me for being absent. I want him hating me for being me.

Jackie: I think that you, you have to, should slow down. You should think this through. This is a *huge* step. . . . You are the only thing standing between me and . . .

Following an interruption when a nurse enters the room with O'Hara's baby, Jackie then embraces O'Hara who is now holding the baby. Despite such a close sense of resolution, the enduring narrative is one of isolation, that Jackie will be lost without O'Hara, who appears like a parent to Jackie, as much as to her new child. It is notable that Jackie highlights the significance of work, as a substitute for the domestic, affirming that: "There are all kinds of people here who depend on you". However through Jackie taking on the role of the child, in many ways she blurs her sense of identity, seeming incongruous, as she is both mother and child. This is particularly significant in the close of this scene, as Jackie is represented alongside O'Hara's real child, engendering Jackie as the queer child.

As Kathryn Bond Stockton tells us with regards to the queer child, and the notion of childhood identity:

> We should start again with the problem of the child as a general idea. The child is precisely who we are not and, in fact, never were. It is the act of adults looking back. It is a ghostly, and reachable fancy.
>
> (p. 5)

Hence the representation of the child is an ideal. This is particularly significant within the representation of Jackie as a childlike figure needing support from O'Hara, as O'Hara's real child displaces her, and Jackie is the ghostlike queer child. As Lee Edelman (2004) defines youth and the impossibility of queer desire: "queerness can never define an identity; it can only ever disturb one" (p. 17). Hence through Jackie appearing as a "queer" child, she is both mother and child in one complex identity. She offers a disturbing representation not that dissimilar to the symbolic pregnant mother, who exists outside the symbolic representational world, seeming incongruous, rather than fully formed.

This sense of incongruity, I argue however, does not necessarily devalue Jackie's discourse; rather it frames her emotional universe, and the extents of her needs. This is particularly significant in the relationship between Antoinette and Jackie (see Figure 2.1), which seems more equally balanced.

Figure 2.1 Julie White as Antoinette (left) confronts Edie Falco as Jackie Peyton (right) in a scene from *Nurse Jackie*, series 6.

Showtime, screenshot.

Whilst there are aspects of support from Antoinette to Jackie, seeming like a mother, in many ways they are both childlike. For example, not only does Antoinette attempt to gain trust from Jackie by assuring her that they are both similarly addicts who potentially could relapse, she is also willing to make herself vulnerable, in the hope that they can communicate, and improvements will be made. Whilst O'Hara is willing to support Jackie emotionally and financially, the extent of Antoinette's vulnerability is more profound, as she is an addict herself.

For example when Jackie feels threatened by Antoinette, for fear that Antoinette may reveal to her workplace colleagues that she is taking drugs again, Jackie capitalises on their imagined equality as potential drug addicts, likely to relapse. In a pivotal sequence Jackie and Antoinette meet at a bar, and they discuss their psychological states. Antoinette advises that she is prone to relapse of alcohol addiction, as she had slept with Eddie (the pharmacist that had been Jackie's drug supplier, and Jackie's ex lover), and Antoinette feels depressed. Jackie tells Antoinette that she is fed up with her boyfriend Frank for not understanding her life as an addict, putting her mobile phone in a jug of water when her rings her.

Antoinette:	We are in really sorry shape. I think we should just move in together—pull some *Laverne and Shirley* shit. . . .
Jackie:	Maybe I am coming around [to rehab]. Maybe we could go in together. It would be nice to go in with someone, less lonely. . . .
Jackie:	My drink. [Takes pill, swallowing it whole] If I'm going to rehab, I'm going there high.
Antoinette:	Waiter can I have a Sidecar with Cointreau, sugar rim. Fuck *Laverne and Shirley*; let's go all *Thelma and Louise*.
Jackie:	Didn't they drive off a cliff?
Antoinette:	Oh I forgot that part . . . just remembered all the fun bits.
Jackie:	Who forgets the ending?
Antoinette:	Alcoholics! Been waiting 10 years for this. If I'm going off a cliff I'm going off a cliff I am going with yah.

Jackie and Antoinette seem like old friends about to go on the journey of a lifetime. However in referring the 1970s retro situation comedy depicting the 1960s about best friends *Shirley and Laverne* (1976–83) alongside the 1990s tragic feminist road movie *Thelma and Louise* (1991), an uneasy juxtaposition is provided which suggests an unhappy end. This is proven to be true, when after a journey to the rehab centre, Jackie just books in Antoinette, professing no knowledge that they had agreed to go to rehab together. She simply states to the receptionist that it takes all means to get addicts into rehab. In response, unsurprisingly Antoinette feels humiliated and totally let down, that after ten years sober, she had made herself vulnerable to help Jackie, yet this had been a trick to disempower Antoinette, so Jackie could feel safe at work, and she could keep on taking drugs.

Seeming like equals, and best friends, but in fact acting like lost children progressing through adolescence, this sequence foregrounds the naivety of Antoinette, who acted like the trusting child, hoping that through camaraderie she could help her friend. While Jackie is represented as satisfied with her despatch of Antoinette, our attention is drawn to the need for belonging, mostly exhibited by Antoinette, and the loss and sense of betrayal that she experiences. At the same time aspects of belonging and camaraderie are counterpointed with abject notions of self-preservation, placing the individual centre stage rather than the community or the coupling.

The representation of Jackie in this way highlights the addict's sense of ego depletion, and behavioural issues that surround this. As Candice L. Shelby (2016) tells us:

> [I]f people experience too much stress will have too many demands requiring self-control, they will have diminished resources available for resisting temptations. . . . [T]he ego depletion model, seeing relapse in terms of a shift in judgement brought on by exhausted stories of energy for self-control, can explain distal activity [within] addiction as end means of reasoning of the usual kind, engaged in once the decision to use is made.
>
> (pp. 55–57)

Hence Jackie's decision to prioritise drug use over friendship or support potentially concerns her need to maintain her ego, as a health professional, who might be valued within the workplace. Under stress to resist drugs, and take control through going to rehab, she is exhausted, and sees the only means of recovery as to nourish her ego, that not only can she continue to do her job that she is valued for, but that she is able to deal with threats to her ego or her status, evident in the challenge of Antoinette. Notably as Jackie leaves Antoinette at rehab with Antoinette bleakly stating that Jackie is a "cunt" and that she never wants to see her again, as Jackie walks down the street, she smiles and seems to bask in glory, appearing thrilled that she has vanquished her imagined foe.

The shift of Antoinette from ideal sponsor and mother-like figure to Jackie, to potential captor and judge, reveals the eco-centric nature of Jackie's relationship with people. Through attempting to get support from Dr O'Hara who appears as a mother substitute, and through torturing Antoinette in the manner that children play tricks on and humiliate imagined foes,

Jackie plays the role of the victim seeming as a child and an adolescent, not fully formed, but concerned for self-preservation, in that moment.

Despite this egocentric abject focus on self-preservation, seeming more of a child than a mother, she demonstrates the ability to be a caring parent, evident in her relationship with Zoey at work and Charlie, a fellow drug addict. Hence while she appears as an absent or unstable mother with regard to her relationship with her own children Fiona and Grace, her metaphorical family ties to her symbolic children seem more fully developed.

For example Jackie is valued by Zoey often involving mentoring that seems more maternal, rather than professional (see Figure 2.2). In the pilot episode when Zoey is unsure of her ability to do the job, further discouraged after bringing in food to share with her colleagues, Jackie makes a statement:

> What's this about, nobody ate your muffins? You found an ear in the toilet? So what! You know what this job is honey? This job is about wading through a shit storm of people who come into this place on the very worst day of their life. Just so you know doctors are here to diagnose. Not heal, we heal! All Saints is in the business of flipping beds, that's it, end of story. The fact that you have the slightest inclination to help people puts you miles ahead of 100% of the population. So buck up, stop crying. If you need to cry go to the ladies room.

Figure 2.2 Merritt Weaver as Zoey (left) and Edie Falco as Jackie Peyton (right) in a scene from *Nurse Jackie*, series 2.

Showtime, screenshot.

Juxtaposing the constitution and the politics of the hospital, in relation to the role of doctors and nurses who work there, Jackie raises Zoey's spirits, admitting that there will be times when you might be vulnerable. However rather than discouraging her for her unique possibly awkward sensibility, she highlights Zoey's unique ability to care for people. In her role as a nurse, Jackie presents a maternal figure to Zoey, in many ways encouraging emotional as much as professional ability.

Added to this the representation of 17-year-old Charlie, a fellow inmate when Jackie goes to rehab in season 4, emulates a mother and child relationship. Unable to get close to her own children (Grace and Fiona), Charlie appears as a child that she understands. A sense of camaraderie is presented in the manner that seemed apparent between Antoinette and Jackie, offering the ability to share stories of drug use. However while Antoinette was in recovery (before the relapse encouraged by Jackie) Charlie appears as the damaged child that she needs to care for, and is highly prone to suicide. Unlike her own child Grace who she feels guilty about for failing to identify with her when she was young, Charlie is a mirror vision of her own addict's life. Jackie and Charlie bond in a way that adolescents might bond, however because Charlie offers no threat to Jackie, but simply is a reminder of her own poor behaviour, she cares for him, as she should care for herself.

Notably, when Charlie eventually passes away from a drug overdose, and Jackie is with him on his deathbed, alongside his father Dr Cruz, juxtaposition is made to Dr O'Hara giving birth, which takes place at the same time in a different part of the hospital. Life and death are represented as coexistent, with Jackie switching between the instance of Charlie's death, and the instance of O'Hara's son's birth, seeming to occur at the same moment. Jackie shifts between life and death scenarios. This however, I argue is not a metaphor for the choices that Jackie must make, but rather frames her liminality as between places. This is particularly evident, after the death of Charlie, when she continues to communicate with him through her mobile phone, leaving messages on his answerphone. She imagines that he is still alive, and he acts as a therapeutic source of identification. She is able to discuss the problems that she has, imagining that he is still there for her. However this frames Jackie's inability to move on, as much as offering her some sense of meaningful solace. In this sense Jackie is represented not only as a mother and as a child, but also as a figure that is between places, unable to find a way forward. While the representation of Jackie, respectively, with both Zoey and Charlie as part of the metaphorical family, offers a deep sense of maternal care that seems more vivid than the relationship she has with her own children, in effect these are signifiers of her status as the "absent mother" as theorised by Susan Harwood. The absent mother's punishment is that she will be defined as alien within the domestic environment. The American Dream becomes the domestic nightmare, which in Jackie's case is doubly abject for her distraction to work and to opiate addiction.

Conclusion

Like the notion of "manifest destiny" inherent in the American Dream that assures us that a new place exists where happiness will be found, and it is ours to take, *Nurse Jackie* offers a complex vision of identity formation and aspiration. We know that the destiny of Jackie Peyton may not just involve a rough road ahead leading to a new place of imagined comfort and leisure, but also that her chosen journey is precipitous, possibly involving endurance, deceit and demise. For Jackie the American Dream is a subliminal world of feelings and emotions, desires and tribulations, largely made vivid through her addition to opiates. Her identity as a mother operating within the physical consumer- and work-oriented American Dream equally is problematic, as she is largely ineffective in the domestic environment, and she relies on metaphorical family relationships, to affirm her identity as a mother. *Nurse Jackie* situates its titular character of Jackie Peyton, as both working for the dream, but also living in the nightmare, ultimately not finding that secure place.

However, as a product of situation comedy and as an exemplar of quality television, *Nurse Jackie* frames the significance of the American Dream as a context of engagement, and as a means to move forward. Despite this Jackie Peyton's identity as an absent mother, seeming childlike and adolescent, under stress in managing her ego depletion, offers the prospect of a malevolent form. While we are aware that Jackie is responding to her condition, as an addict, assigned to a life of urges, needs and self-preservation, at the same time we begin to understand the complexity of her life, in meeting expectations and in taking on roles. *Nurse Jackie* is not just an absent mother failing at living the American Dream; she is a metaphorical touchstone, offering a site of identification that might encourage a deeper understanding.

However *Nurse Jackie*'s narrative arc, in relation to televisual form, is only part of the story. As we shall see in the next chapter, the iconic identity of Edie Falco in playing Jackie Peyton, and scriptwriters such as Liz Brixius, Linda Wallem and Clyde Phillips, place their personal lives within the cultural frame, in stimulating audience identification.

3 Edie Falco and Star Persona

Introduction

In an interview for the Archive of American Television (AAT 2018), Edie Falco, star of the television series *Nurse Jackie* (2009–15), states:

> I want the stuff that I do to be reminiscent of experiences that I've had in real life, rather than some idealised version of another person that no one can ever live up to.

In an intense, developed and wide-ranged interview (lasting for over two hours) that considers her personal ambitions, professional strategies and skills, Edie Falco makes a connection between her real-life experiences and the nature of the roles that she performs, suggesting a kind of realism. Through framing a need for personal resonance and authenticity, Falco suggests that her star persona is informed as much by her professional ability as her life experiences and political visions.

This chapter consequently explores the professional identity of Edie Falco as an actress, considering the formulation of her star persona, and the utilisation of her celebrity identity in providing an artistic, cultural and political vision. I also contextualise the professional identities of the scriptwriters and show runners, involved in the production of *Nurse Jackie*, including Liz Brixius, Linda Wallem and Clyde Phillips as celebrities in their own right, where they contextualise the potential of Edie Falco. Central within this is Edie Falco's ability to suggest an authenticity, and a personal/political vision, with regards to her representation of drug addiction. As part of this Edie Falco's star persona involves aspects of self-reflexivity, framing the notion of the "mutable self" (Zurcher 1977), evident in her willingness to reveal deeper contexts of her vulnerability. The star persona of Edie Falco represents an entertainment commodity of the media industry, which is relevant not only within her foundational texts such as *Oz, The Sopranos* and *Nurse Jackie*, but also is apparent in her guest appearances or short-term roles, such as within *30 Rock*, and in *Law & Order True Crime: The Menendez Murders*. I argue that these texts frame Falco's performative star persona.

Star Emergence

Edie Falco has appeared in quite a few notable films, including *Laws of Gravity* (1992), *Sunshine State* (2002), *Freedomland* (2006), *3 Backyards* (2011) and more recently *Outside In* (2018), offering sophisticated performances while working with progressive directors/writers such as Nick Gomez, John Sayles, Joe Roth, Eric Mendelsohn and Lynn Shelton.[1] Despite such progressive work, mostly in independent film, her star persona emerged from her work within television drama, specifically associated with her appearance as Carmela Soprano in *The Sopranos* (1999–2007). Prior to *The Sopranos*, Falco had not only frequently taken on recurring roles in the drama series *Law & Order* (1990–), *Homicide: Life on the Street* (1993–99) and *New York Undercover* (1994–98), but also her appearance in the controversial TV prison drama *Oz* (1997–2003) as a recurring cast member, I argue, offers a clear foundation to her emerging star identity within televisual form.

Produced for HBO, who later developed *The Sopranos*, *Oz* frames Edie Falco as a regular character within the prison drama cast. Appearing as the character of Diane Whittlesey who is a correctional officer within the Oswald Maximum Security Facility, she is represented as a single mother, who has experience of spousal, and substance, abuse. At the same time as a hard worker, who also cares for her mother besides her young daughter, she is represented as a strong and resourceful figure within workplace and domestic settings. Significantly the context of *Oz* offered a counter cultural setting for Edie Falco's identity. As Joe Wlodarz (2005) tells us

> *Oz* was unrelenting in its attention to prison violence and conflicts of identity, but it was also a remarkably innovative and compelling prison drama that thoroughly indicted the prison industrial complex and broke new ground in the representation of racial and sexual diversity on television.
>
> (pp. 59–60)

As a co-creation between Tom Fontana who had been a writer on *Homicide: Life on the Street* (where he had worked with Falco) and film director Barry Levinson whose work included the celebrated *Rain Man* (1988), *Oz* may be considered as a hybrid cultural form, developing links between TV and film that offered a new sense of "postmodern" realism. Appealing to the subscription channel HBO who was looking for "a dramatic series that would complement its acclaimed, if often disturbing documentary series *America Undercover* and the success of its prison based documentaries such as *Lock Up: The Prisoners of Rikers Island* (1994)" (Wlodarz 2005, p. 64), *Oz* became a platform that challenged hierarchical notions of narrative, in the manner of postmodernity. Notably as *Oz* "lacked any clear heroes, victories and moral messages" (Wlodarz 2005, p. 64), a sense of democracy was present in its ability to foreground diverse characters connected to race, gender, sexuality and ethnicity. Hence rather than following traditional narrative arcs that may highlight clear moral codes, prioritising white identity, heterosexuality and monogamy, a complex moral universe is presented, where the audience are encouraged to question normative hierarchies. As part of this, although Falco's character within the series presents depth through caring for her mother and daughter, the general narrative landscape within the series foregrounds "flawed protagonists" and the significance of the antihero.

For example, in season 1 of *Oz* (Ep. 4 "Capital P") which focuses on an inmate execution, Edie Falco's character of Diane Whittlesey and fellow prison worker Tim McManus (played by Terry Kinney) are in intimate conversation. Diane recalls of a time when she was married and she wanted to go deer hunting with her husband, from whom she is now divorced. She recalls how she was exited to shoot the deer, but when she went over to see the results of her actions, she felt deep emotions (see Figure 3.1):

> And this deer looked up to me with these eyes. These eyes like flashlights. I knelt beside it and I held its head, and I whispered: "I am sorry". Then like batteries going bad, the light in his eyes flickered a little bit, and ah, went out. For the next two years that we were married every time that I walked into the den, I had to stare at that fucking deer's dead eyes. I had to dust them. When we got divorced all that I asked for, the deer's head, and I buried it.

Linking the execution of a prisoner with the death of a deer, Diane Whittlesey represents an antihero in her complex emotional response to the death of the animal. Offering humanistic and humane empathetic performance in respecting animals as much as people, Falco's representation of the antihero frames issues of guilt, responsibility and intuitive emotion.

As Amanda Lotz (2014) advises, the antihero within literature is a character "who lacks the attributes of the traditional protagonist or hero, such as courage, honesty or grace" (p. 63), however may reveal complex emotional integrity, or at least force. For example, Milly Buonnanno (2017) considers

Figure 3.1 Edie Falco as Diane Whittlesey in *Oz*, series 1, episode 4 "Capital P".
HBO, screenshot.

the rise of the television antihero stemming from the representation of Mafia
boss Tony Soprano (played by James Gandolfini), within *The Sopranos*.
Tony Soprano is a complex antihero as he is not only a Mafia boss involved
in the crime industry, but also he is a relatively dedicated family man, and
is in therapy. At the same time his wife Carmela Soprano, played by Edie
Falco, is considered as an early exemplar of the "female anti-hero", for her
strong female character and relative moral ambiguity (discussed below).
However, I argue that Falco's appearance in *Oz* may be considered as an
earlier representation of the female antihero, where the personal is more
central than the ordered or simply heroic.

I argue that Edie Falco's emerging star persona, within *Oz*, not only set
a precedent for the notion of the female anti-heroine, but also offers a contextual relationship with the production company HBO and the creators of
the series, TV screenwriter Tom Fontana and film director Barry Levinson.
The relationship to HBO is central, as a leading media production company
which offered new scope in commissioning new dramatic content that was
inspired by crime and prison documentaries. The involvement of leading
scriptwriting and production figures known for hard hitting and complex

crime drama offered a production framework for Falco's star persona. As part of this the media audience are encouraged to identify Falco's commodity identity as working within *Oz*, as a relatively new postmodern social realist crime drama, that could be seen as a precursor to quality television (see Chapter 2).

Edie Falco's star persona was established with *Oz* as the character of Diane Whittlesey, later developing within *The Sopranos* as Carmela Soprano (discussed further below) and then advanced furthermore within *Nurse Jackie* as Jackie Peyton. While she has appeared in a diverse range of media texts besides these (discussed above and further below), I argue that as a main character, or as a leading character, in *Oz*, *The Sopranos* and *Nurse Jackie*, her identity is consistently framed as an anti-heroine within quality television. Falco's star persona is a commodity of media form; also it involves aspects of personal identity that may be traced to her personal goals.

Reflexivity and Autobiographical Self

As Richard Dyer (1986) tells us:

> Stars are involved in making themselves into commodities; they are both labour and the thing that labour produces. . . . The people who do this labour include the star him/herself as well as make-up artist, hairdressers, dress designers, dieticians, bodybuilding coaches, acting, answering and other teachers, publicists, pinup photographs, gossip columnist, and so on. . . . Stars are examples of the way people live their relation to production in capitalist society.
>
> (pp. 5–6)

Edie Falco is a star persona that exists as a unit of media commodity, relative to aspects of labour, and consumption. Her appearances in media products such as *Oz*, *The Sopranos* and *Nurse Jackie* are on the one hand related to her skills as an actor and how audiences may read her cultural, social or artistic value, and on the other, her star identity involves a need to reproduce that identity and involves stimulating more productions that in some way replicate or utilise key features that have been successful in selling the product of the star.

Edie Falco's star identity is framed within certain cultural and social signifiers. As an exemplar, or emerging model as an anti-heroine within *Oz*, in some senses signifying vulnerability and otherness, and as a female situated in a masculine world (the male prison), she is related to notions of strength and resolve within complex or oppressive circumstances. Notably this was particularly evident in considering Falco's later and more well-known role in *The Sopranos*, where as a wife of a Mafia boss, as Carmela Soprano, her character has to contend not only again with a male-oriented, crime-based narrative world, but also in some sense she is isolated, despite female friendship and family networks. In this sense, her developing star identity within *The Sopranos* continues to reinforce her identity as a strong woman, existing in a complex moral universe, where she is largely subject to the power of men.

For example, in the final episode of the first season of *The Sopranos* entitled "I Dream of Jeannie Cusamano", Carmela and Father Phil (the local priest she has a close friendship with) are in conversation, after he comes to Carmela's house with food and a DVD. Father Phil discusses Carmela's husband Tony, who Father Phil wants to face up to his actions, as a criminal.[2]

Father Phil: As I was saying my real concern for Tony. . .

Carmela: Father, he doesn't give a flying fuck! You know it, and I know it, at least for the foreseeable future. . . . He's a sinner father, and you come up here and eat his steaks, and you use his home entertainment centre.

Father Phil: The DVD is for you.

Carmela: Really? Even after last week I told you I'm not a big Rene Zellweger fan. . . . If you want to watch *One True Thing* fine, at least admit it. . . . Jesus, you know I get exactly the same thing: "Who Me?" shit—with Tony. Two I don't need!

Carmela calls into question the motives of Father Phil, who she immediately challenges after this exchange for developing unhealthy relationships with needy women (considering herself among these), that he may find sexually arousing. Carmela's challenge to her priest, who to some degree is a confidant to her, and her critique of her husband in the same conversation, frames her character's confidence. By signifying Father Phil and Tony as both childlike, in their inability to admit their motives, which in the case of Father Phil involves an interest in female-oriented romantic films and possibly dubious sexual pleasure, she is articulate and confident, challenging masculine authority. At the same time, she frames the irony of Father Phil's concerns, suggesting hypocrisy, in attempting to judge Tony.

However this challenge to masculine authority is complex. As Kim Akass and Janet McCabe (2017) state:

No one could ever claim Carmela as a role model for contemporary feminism, but neither should anyone dismiss her ability to navigate androcentric hierarchies and highly coded patriarchal worlds to emerge as a formidable figure in her own right.

(p. 67)

While the character of Carmela may appear unlike a feminist, and more like a post feminist (Ganz and Brabon 2018) accepting the reductive status of the female, at the same time her ability to challenge male authority is apparent. However, I argue such a challenge may be apparent not purely in relying on the discourse of the script, but largely in considering Edie Falco's personal investment in the roles that she plays.

While Edie Falco suggested largely that she did not influence the narratives within *The Sopranos* (AAT 2018) unlike her influence on *Nurse Jackie*, she testifies a certain approach in taking on roles, with regard to performance engagement.

> I felt permission to adopt qualities that I wish I had in my real life but felt that I couldn't sustain on a continuous level as a human, but I could do it within the boundaries of the story.
>
> (AAT 2018)

Falco's immersion with the character reveals a sense of investment that highlights a personal need, to almost inhabit the character in a therapeutic sense. Whilst her rendition of Carmela Soprano might not so closely be traced to her personal experience, her rendition of Jackie Peyton in *Nurse Jackie* offers more personal and autobiographical scope.

For example, within the documentary that accompanies the sixth season of *Nurse Jackie*, Edie Falco states:

> I don't know how we are starting season seven, nor do I know how it will end, ultimately whenever it does. All I want is to portray accurately my experience of addiction. The fact that audiences go through that thing that friends and lovers of addicts go through is exactly what I would want to happen.

Considering a need to portray a personal knowledge of addiction within the performative fictional representation I argue not only blurs a distinction between public and private worlds, but also frames a sense of autobiography that is rarely attached to a drama performance. Falco is invested in portraying Jackie Peyton, not only as a strong character, but also wants to invest something of herself within her performance. I argue that her star persona particularly breaks down barriers between public and private lives.

As Richard Dyer tells us, in his landmark book *Heavenly Bodies*: "The private self is . . . represented through a set of oppositions that stem from the division of the world into private and public spaces" (p. 11). With a suggestion that oppositions such as "private/public", "individual/society", "body/brain" often lead audiences to prioritise the emotional knowledge of the star as stemming from the former, seeming to offer access to the private individual body of the star. As Dyer goes on to tell us, considering the impact of Hollywood stars Judy Garland, Paul Robeson and Marilyn Monroe, stars "who are thought to be genuine, who reveal their inner lives, [frame the] genuineness [of] the human body itself" (p. 13). Edie Falco's relationship to the notion of genuineness is highly evident, in her ability to frame her autobiographical narrative, as a survivor of alcohol addiction. As part of this, I argue that her star persona offers a profound self-reflexive nature that frames her vulnerability, as much as her strength.

This might be related to Louis A. Zurcher's (1977) notion of the "mutable self" where issues of instability may be seen as productive within self-construction, revealing that "the self may gain coherence by being in constant movement" (Rinkin 2000, p. 5). Through Edie Falco revealing her vulnerability as a survivor of alcohol addiction, who admits that you never recover from addiction, but must live with it, she frames her vulnerable potential. Rather than offering a simplistic vision of self as recovered or repaired, a focus is made upon the "reflexive project of the self" (Giddens 1992) where individuals exhibit their personal emotions and feelings, providing "new storytelling" (Pullen 2012).

Such a process is indicative of contemporary "risk society", which Ulrich Beck (1992) argues offers performative potential through individuals exhibiting and sharing their vulnerability. As Zurcher (1977) attests:

> The focal point of self-concept would be process or change itself— stability would become based on change—change would be stability in the same way, metaphorically speaking, as a tornado has substance and stability because of its swirling momentum.
>
> (p. 182)

Edie Falco's desire to reveal her vulnerability offers strength largely though her ability to articulate the finite details of her troubled personal past, and the need to learn from this.

However as Falco tells us:

> I'm sober 25 years, so I have a quite a bit of distance. There was something beautiful about revisiting it [in *Nurse Jackie*] without feeling like it was dangerous. I couldn't have done that show with ten years sobriety. It would not have been pleasant. I'm also a cancer survivor, and I got offered a bunch of scripts about women who had cancer, and I was like, I absolutely can't do this. When I'm too close to the material, it's almost like a kryptonite thing. I just get static and I can't inhabit a different person, maybe because it feels too much like my person.
>
> (Jones 2018)

Hence although Falco is able to use her personal experience, a certain objective distance is needed. Although she has in fact played a woman with cancer in *Horace and Pete* (see Introduction), this was in a supporting role, with a less distinct focus on the experience of the disease.

However with regards to her experience as an ex alcohol addict, Falco offers an eloquent assessment of the character of Jackie Peyton who at the end of season 5 relapses after one year sober, just before testifying her sobriety in the episode:

> The behaviour of addicts defies rational across-the-board, it's usually about as upsetting as it can be. People that you're absolutely sure are on the right straight narrow, will suddenly take a turn at the most unpredictable times. Often times when things are going well the underlying issue being that this person cannot metabolise good news. It's not what they're used to. It doesn't fit their ideas of what they deserve and who they are. Rather and try make sense of it they say "take me out I can't know what to do with the situation".

(AAT 2018)

Through Falco framing the complex psychological depth of her character function relative to her own experiences, she offers a robust identity as self-assured, through working through issues of vulnerability, in the manner of the mutable self. As part of this she frames her life story in the manner of an "autobiographical self" (Pullen 2016b), where she offers a political vision based on her own life experiences.

Star Role Models as "Other" and "Survivor"

Her star persona offers bifurcate potential for identification, in representing her "autobiographical self". On the one hand Falco represents the plight of the addict, offering empathy and understanding to a person who may have felt similar experiences. On the other she represents a triumph of recovery, where she has overcome subjugation as an outsider. As Dyer discusses with regards to Judy Garland, who ultimately died from a drug overdose, for gay men she had represented a sense of survival. Dyer affirms that while gay men identified with Garland as "representing gay men's neurosis and hysteria" (p. 146), later she represented "gay men's resilience in the face of oppression" (p. 146).

Likewise we may consider that Edie Falco's representation as Jackie Peyton, who identifies with key queer characters in the cast, such as gay males (MoMo played by Haaz Sleiman and Thor played by Stephen Wallem) and female bisexuals (Dr O'Hara played by Eve Best) offers an alliance between straight and queer identities, resisting "disparate and individual senses of abjection . . . working together as a political, cultural and social union" (Pullen 2016a, p. 13). Notably prior to *Nurse Jackie* in 2004, Falco has appeared as a lesbian fictional character in *Will and Grace* (1998–) season 6, in an episode titled "East Side Story", offering an alliance or union with queer audiences. In this brief appearance with Chloë Sevigny as her same-sex partner, the notion of the American Dream and domesticity (see Chapter 2) is parodied, where the couple are represented as sophisticated entrepreneurs and homemakers. Hence Falco's star persona, in a similar manner to Garland, I argue, offers the potential as a survivor role model, resonant to diverse queer audiences. Such identification may be stimulated through her nuanced performativity, which I argue encourages audiences' self-reflection.

This is a theme particularly taken up by the co-creators of *Nurse Jackie* Liz Brixius and Linda Wallem. Notably, in the early stages of promoting the series to audiences, they reflected on their own histories of addiction, and how in many ways they are survivors themselves. However, as part of this, they frame their relation to Edie Falco, as a defining performative factor, rather than exclusively utilising their writing skills.

> Liz Brixius: Edie's [work involves] calibration. She loves nuance. She is the only actress in the world who says, "I want less lines". She wants to play it. . . . Linda and I, when we lived together we would watch *The Sopranos*, and we would rewind Edie's scenes, and she might have only had four minutes of screen time in the 52 minutes, but the impact that she left was so enormous. So we would say imagine if Carmela were the centre or the sun in the universe, and everything were in orbit around her.
> (YouTube 2018d)

Through placing Edie Falco at the centre of the narrative, the scriptwriters utilise her nuanced performance skills, and as a means to offer deeper resonance to their narrative. Capitalising not only on Falco's prior representation within *The Sopranos* as the iconic figure of Carmela, whose performative ability seemed to be captivating, but also on Falco's identity as an actress who has spoken publicly about her own history of addiction (to alcohol), a sense of personal investment is presented.

For example, as Edie Falco tells us in the DVD documentary *Deceit, Descent, Destruction* that accompanies season 6, with regards to her insight into addiction:

> The mind of an addict makes more sense to me than normal people. You know addiction is a very complicated disease, a lot of times it's predisposition to addiction in conjunction with inner pain that you're trying to drown out.

Falco's ability is that her nuanced performance intersects with the notion of inner pain, extending from her own experiences with addiction. Hence in the manner that Richard Dyer (2001) suggests that audiences engage with stars as role models, Brixius and Wallem potentially experienced an intense sense of identification with Falco, where they can read such nuance as representing strength or complexity.

For example, Andrew Tudor (1974) identifies aspects of "emotional infinity" that can emerge in the relationship between public figures and audiences, where the "audience feels a loose attachment to a particular protagonist [stimulating] involvement" (p. 80), and understanding that may connect to their own lives. I argue that Brixius and Wallem as spectators to Falco within *The Sopranos* were well placed to identify with her nuanced performance which iterated survival from addiction, enabling them to identify her suitability in taking on the leading role in *Nurse Jackie*. Not only might they experience an "emotional infinity", where they identify with her as ex addicts themselves and they might read her "inner pain", but also aspects of "imitation" and "projection" may be apparent, where they imagine their life stories reflected in writing the narrative for her within the series. This is not to say that their involvement with Edie Falco is purely based on their star identification with her, but inevitably they might be susceptible to view her this way as suitable to lead *Nurse Jackie*, empathising with her as an icon of female strength and survival.

Celebrity and Form

Liz Brixius and Linda Wallem share life stories of personal addiction, and seem to possess common educational goals with Edie Falco. Despite this, after Brixius's and Wallem's departure from *Nurse Jackie* after season 4, while Edie Falco remains as the only explicit icon of addiction within the production team, a sense of momentum continued under the leadership of Clyde Phillips. Notably Phillips had previously worked on the Showtime series *Dexter* (2006–13), which as a macabre postmodern crime drama that focused on a serial killer who actually was a forensic technician, seemed to offer a similar sense of irony and parody as *Nurse Jackie*, even if it did not share a generic similarity. Although Martha Nochimson (2018) suggests that the impact of Phillips was reductive, testifying that "the series was forced back into the mould of conventional narrative, and the women were newly objectified", it is clear that Falco not only remained a key force in directing the character of Jackie Peyton in regards to tone, performance and narrative outcomes for that character (see AAT 2018), but also that Phillips himself was invested in the star potential of Falco as a guiding force.

As Clyde Phillips stated, not that long after becoming the show runner:

> [Edie] can give us back anything we want, only better. As a writer I believe it's my challenge to take emotions, and turn them into words, and then have an actor, take those words and turn them back into emotions, only better. Boy does Edie do that!
>
> (YouTube 2018e)

In a similar manner that Brixius and Wallem discuss Falco's ability for nuance in performativity, Phillips considers her interpretive skills as exceptional, particularly with regards to the conveyance of emotions. Despite this, in some sense this emotional landscape altered within *Nurse Jackie*, after the arrival of Phillips.

For example, Phillips had plans to modify the tone and the form of the series.

> I had been watching *Nurse Jackie*, [but I feel] it kind of lost its comedy roots. And one of the conversations that I had with Showtime was: Let's make this a dark comedy again. Let's make it edgy again. Let's make it sexy again. Let's make it premium cable again.
>
> (YouTube 2018e)

By framing the comedic nature of *Nurse Jackie*, Phillips implies a return to a focus on irony, a key element of *Dexter*—albeit in a different context. At the same time, with an iteration that there was a need to return the values of "premium cable", foregrounding "sexiness" and "edginess", a sense of commodity is implied as much as provocation. Notably premium cable producer Showtime had prior success with series that had focused on controversy or explicit sex, apparent in *Queer as Folk* (2000–05) and *The L World* (2004–09). These shows were provocative in their representation of LGBT communities, at the same time their focus on sexual acts as much as sexual community offered provocation as much as political intent.

Under the leadership of Clyde Phillips *Nurse Jackie* seemed to be more provocative. This involved not only more representations of drug-taking culture, and references to the impact on family and peers, but also the depths of depravity became more fully formed. I argue that the character of Jackie Peyton increasingly becomes more unsalvageable, and part of this involves a deeper, more raw performance from Edie Falco in playing the role that in some senses, tests the boundaries of empathy and identification.

For example, although the character of Jackie Peyton in the first four seasons had proven to be a morally problematic character in terms of her failure to be loyal to her partner, or to be loyal to her colleagues or to be loyal to her workplace in following correct procedure, her culpability was often offset with the positive outcomes of her good deeds, relative to the strength of her character. For example, she may have saved someone's life albeit by dubious means, or she may have appeared strong and sophisticated in her conviction to do good work. However, from season 5 Jackie Peyton becomes more unstable, and a less likeable character, following the stereotypical downfall of the addict in the later stages of addiction. As part of this she sometimes appears as morally reprehensible. This is evident in season 6, when she has sex with a drug dealer in the toilets, whilst her boyfriend Frank is singing karaoke at a barn dance (Season 6, Ep. 2); and in another instance it is evident when she encourages a dying patient to take the responsibility for an identity fraud drug related crime that she committed (Season 6, Ep. 11, see also Chapter 4). In this way Edie Falco, playing the role of Jackie Peyton, tests the endurances of the audience to like her character, as she frames abject contemptibility and depravity. However Falco recognises the need for a kind of unpleasant realism, in the representation of Jackie Peyton:

> It wouldn't necessarily serve me with a show I think if I was thinking in terms of making her likeable. By the time [addicts are] in the throes of low parts of their addiction, they are not likeable.
>
> (*Nurse Jackie* DVD documentary *Deceit, Descent, Destruction*)

Hence through Falco, closely mapping the descending moral universe of the addict, who is unable to recover, a sense of heightened realism is offered.

While it is possible to argue that this representational depravity could be overemphasised in the manner that Stuart Hall (1997) considers the notion of disavowal, where an audience may be intensely interested in the addict as "the other" as entertainment, and they may not necessarily learn from this, Edie Falco's performative ability is central. Edie Falco's nuanced rendition, I argue, enables a more sophisticated reading of the performative potential. For example, just after the character of Jackie Peyton has had sex with a drug dealer in the toilets (as discussed above), it is important to note that our focus is not necessarily on the details of the sex act itself, but rather the convergence of the performance occurs a little after. When we see Jackie Peyton high on drugs dancing in front of her boyfriend, who had been singing karaoke all along while she was having sex in the toilet, Falco dances in a childlike carefreeness, and her face seems resplendent with glory. Such a nuanced convergence frames not simply the provocation of the narrative, but the subtlety of the actor's emotional skills in conveying a psychological moment, which frames the character's vulnerability as much as the depravity.

However Edie Falco's performative ability is not only relevant in the key texts where she leads, but also it is apparent where she appears in less substantial roles, that whilst might seem subordinate, I argue offer deep resonance.

Performativity

Notably as a recurring guest within *30 Rock* (2006–13) within the second season (in 2007), and as a leading actress in *Law & Order True Crime: The Menendez Murders* (2017), her star persona identity appears as equally vivid, in context to the key roles that she is known for, such as in *Oz*, *The Sopranos* and *Nurse Jackie*. The narratives of these texts are entirely disparate, as in *30 Rock* Falco plays a fictional Democrat politician who falls hopelessly in love with a media mogul who is a Republican, and in *The Menendez Murders* she plays a celebrated real-life lawyer who defends two brothers accused of murdering their parents who allegedly sexually abused them. However, I have selected these not so much for their congruity within Falco's oeuvre, but for their ability to frame aspects of her star persona.

As part of this, a key aspect in Edie Falco's approach to her work is her ability to inhabit a character, contextualising her own identity or feelings. Notably Falco tells us:

> Some of the biggest emotions that I felt in my life were actually in the guise of a different person but they still store themselves in my body so I feel like I experienced that, and I did.
>
> (AAT 2018)

Falco's relationship to her roles within *30 Rock* and *The Menendez Murders* is complex. In the former Falco admits that she found this role unusual, not so much for the narrative, but in relation to the timing of the comedic performance, admitting that she was in awe of the main cast for their rhythm and speed in delivering the narrative, and saw this as a world apart from her work (AAT 2018). In the latter Falco clearly identified with the political and cultural narrative of child abuse and crime, but admitted that she was unconcerned that she had no contact with the real-life person that she was playing (attorney Leslie Abraham) in order to assess the sense of historical authenticity. Hence Falco approached both these roles in the manner that she approached *Nurse Jackie*, *The Sopranos* and *Oz*, that she was less concerned to know the exactitude of the real-life historical event or social worlds, or to need to copy the rules of the dominant forms, but she was willing to learn by intuition, as an individual invested in the cultural context of these roles. As Peggy Phelan (1993) tells us:

> Performance is the art form which most fully understands the generative possibilities of disappearance. Poised for ever at the threshold of the present, performance enacts the productive appeal of the non-reproductive. Trying to suggest that the disappearance of the external other is the means by which self-assurance is achieved requires that one analyse the potential payoffs in such disappearance: performance exposes some of them.
>
> (p. 27)

As Phelan suggests, the notion of performance is a complex process involving immersion into a role suggesting invisibility of the actor, but also some sense of visibility, where aspects of the actor's identity, or the nuance of the performance, intimate the life world of the actor themselves.

While it would seem more likely that Edie Falco may be more "visible" in *The Menendez Murders*, as she is more clearly invested in the emotional story of child abuse, I argue that in many ways her persona is more apparent in *30 Rock*, however in some sense as a parody of her life story. For example if you consider the context of the character that she is playing in *30 Rock*, Celeste Cunningham who is nicknamed CC, she is identified as a Democrat politician which seems like a literal representation of Edie Falco; as discussed in the Introduction she is an proactive Democrat supporter who actively opposes the Republicans (Daily Kos 2018).

Added to this, the real-life celebrity of Falco is parodied in the backstory of her character's rise to fame. For example, in an exchange between new lovers Democrat politician CC and Republican media mogul Jack Donaghy (played by Alec Baldwin), they make fun of politics, where Jack denigrates CC for her admission that she had been working on Hilary Clinton's healthcare package with "God, I want to kiss you on the mouth for saying such ridiculous things". Also Edie's identity with stardom is referenced where CC (played by Edie) admits how she got into politics in a conversation with Jack:

CC: In 1998, I got shot in the face by my neighbour's dog. . . . My neighbour had a Riverton hunting rifle with a faulty trigger safety. The Jack Russell terrier started chewing the area. The gun went off and shot me in the face.

Jack: No! A terrier?

CC: I did what was right. I sued Riverton, my neighbour and the dog. . . . After six reconstructive surgeries, at least I'm better looking now than I used to be.

This exchange is followed with CC proudly stating that as a result, a Lifetime (biographical) movie was made of the story entitled *A Dog Took My Face and Gave Me a Better Face to Change the World.* Through parodying Democrat politics with relation to the (unsafe) proliferation of firearms (a Republican core value), alongside notions of litigation and plastic surgery (as references to American society), a comedic critique is presented that frames the notion of celebrity, evident in the biographical film. While this does not closely map Edie Falco's personal identity, they are ironic references to politics and celebrity. As part of this, the humour comes not so much from the narrative, but the nuanced facial performance given by Falco. She presents a deadpan facial image, seemingly to punctuate the narrative with the movement of her head and eyes, ignoring the obvious comedic narrative of a dog shooting a gun.

While a sense of artifice and parody are central in our reading of Edie Falco in *30 Rock*, elements of artifice are similarly apparent within *The Menendez Murders*, however with a focus on fashion, and a deeper sense of emotional politics. Most notably Edie Falco's appearance in the role of Leslie Abrahamson seems out of character with her previous roles. Largely this might be evident in the form of her hair, where she appears in a large permanent wave blonde wig (see Figure 3.2). Although Falco admits in playing the role that was set in the 1990s that it had been fashionable and she had

Figure 3.2 Edie Falco as Leslie Abrahamson in *Law & Order: True Crime—The Menendez Murders.*

NBC. Image courtesy of Justin Lubin.

wanted her hair in this style (YouTube 2018c), a sense of the unreal or the unusual is apparent in seeing Edie Falco in this way. This is apparent, as in her foundational roles (*Oz*, *The Sopranos* and *Nurse Jackie*); largely she has consistently been "trademarked" with straight blonde hair, of varying lengths. Hence her "other-worldly" appearance in a complex permed wig offers a sense of artifice that challenges the regular way that she has been presented, iterating connections to production as much as representing an authentic historical fashion. As Nicole Pajer (2018) reports in interviewing Anthony Veader, head of hair styling on *The Menendez Murders*:

> Veader also revealed that the bigger ticket wigs, like Falco's, also require the most preparation and storage efforts. . . . Since the wigs are being constantly shampooed or styled, you have to make sure you're not stretching out the lace. It has to constantly fit them perfectly, like a glove, he adds.

The commodity of the "unusual wig", in many ways acts as a character in itself. But at the same time it is maintained with a constant focus on the fit to the actor wearing it, suggesting a sense of authenticity, or believability. However Falco's wig is not only of very high quality, in some senses it is an artwork, with very clearly defined permanent waves (almost like ringlets) that appear iridescent, quite unlike the hair of the real Leslie Abramson, which appears as more dense and less defined. In this way, I argue, the producers of *The Menendez Murders* draw attention to the hair, as a way of parodying or contextualising the star persona of Falco. They do not copy her trademark style, but construct a hybridised "otherworldly" permed version. This is particularly ironic as Falco herself identifies the character of Leslie Abramson as someone who potentially did not care about looking stylish (YouTube 2018b), and in this detail the producers avoid a sense of authenticity/realism that might follow Falco's observation.

Added to this, Falco assesses Abrahamson's performative identity that she was inspired by:

> [Leslie Abrahamson] took the sort of unpopular decision that these people that she is representing, on some level regardless of what they are accused of, are *human*. And I think one of these things that she did, was sort of to humanise them, even just as simply as by touching them [in the court room] on trial. And I think this perturbed people. People don't like to live in that grey area. You know there are good people and bad people, and she was trying to let people imagine, you don't know which is which all the time.
>
> (YouTube 2018b)

Similarly to Edie Falco's rendition of the troubled fictional character of Jackie Peyton, a focus on deferring moral judgement and framing humanity may be seen as a key element that inspired Falco's rendition of Leslie Abrahamson.

For example if we consider a key sequence in the summing up of the trial against the Menendez brothers for murdering their parents, Edie Falco in the role of Leslie Abrahamson cradles the head of Eric Menendez at close of the sequence, and Eric leans in emotionally whispering "thank you". However this humanisation is preceded with a build up, where she frames the imagined crimes of the parents, and the effect on Eric. With photos of the crime scene within the court room that reveal the horror of the murders, Falco as Abrahamson states:

> Where are the photos of Jose Menendez bending his 12 year-old-son over the bed, so that he could "go all the way", in spite of Eric's screams? There is such a picture. Unfortunately, it only exists in Eric's mind. I cannot show you the photos of the crimes that Jose Menendez committed against Eric. But you heard some of the things that he liked to do to his little boy. And one of them was to take tacks like this, and stick them in his thighs. And his butt! And to run needles, along his penis. . . . I don't ask you to pity Eric, but I want you to understand how his childhood put him on a collision course with violence. I want to tell you a story from my life. When I was a child my mother hit me with a wooden coat hanger. I was so mad I hit her back. It was the scariest thing I have ever done in my life. But it happened in an instant, from a wellspring of panic and fear, like this: panic and fear.

Through Edie Falco presenting an intense performative sequence, involving emotional punctuations, where she stabs the notice board with pins, emulating the possible pain that Eric might have been subject to, she walks back and forward to the notice board, as if she herself was in pain, in the manner that a disturbed person paces back and forth, not knowing where to go. At the same time through referencing her own story of instinctive defensive violence against her mother, she opens up her own feelings of shame. Falco's nuanced performance, framing her own seemingly accessible emotional landscape, seems like a story of a mother caring for her own child, asking for the jury to comprehend his vulnerability, and ultimately his humanity. As discussed above through cradling his head at the close of this sequence, she articulates to the jury that Eric is not necessarily a monster, but a frightened and disturbed child.

Edie Falco's performance is intense, seeming like a culmination of her earlier roles, where as a strong woman, she reveals compassion, and strength, but is articulate, rebellious and believable. Her identity is coded not only through her engaging and provocative performance, but also is referenced in the artifice of her hairstyle. In the manner that Falco also performs in *30 Rock*, we read this as an actor playing another great role that might be part of a canon of esteemed works. However, we are reminded that these instances are "performances", where realism is placed in context. Falco's star persona frames such knowingness, as aspects of artifice and realism are part of her performative potential, in many ways framing her public political ideals, as much as her skills in telling a story.

Conclusion

Edie Falco's star persona involves both a focus on her commodity as an actor, and a focus on her personal experiential self. Central within this is her identity as an inspirational actress who presents a powerful female image, established largely within progressive "quality television" drama. Significantly, through taking on roles that have framed the anti-heroine, she has established a body of work that offers sophistication in storytelling. From portraying a female prison manager, to the wife of a Mafia boss, to a nurse addicted to drugs, in *Oz*, *The Sopranos* and *Nurse Jackie* respectively, she has taken on roles that might be seen as unsympathetic. However, through her sophisticated, calibrated and nuanced acting skills, she has provided complex character profiles that have enduring cultural resonance.

Through publicly discussing her personal history of alcohol addiction, particularly with regards to her performance in *Nurse Jackie*, she reveals a vulnerable sense of self, but is intuitive and powerful in the manner of the "mutable self" (Zurcher 1977). Her "autobiographical self" (Pullen 2016b) is inevitably bound up with her ambition to take on certain roles that might be seen as provocative, or controversial. For example her role in *The Menendez Murders* might seem like a regular contribution to a "true life" crime drama, where details, facts and moral outcomes are historicised, to "put the record straight". Despite this, conversely, through her calibrated and nuanced performance, rather she opens up a complex moral universe, where aspects of child sexual abuse and the emotional universe of the victims feature more prominently in asking questions that cannot be resolved.

It is this need for questions, rather than simple answers that dominates Edie Falco's work. Even when taking on what might seem like stock characters in comedy, such as her role in *30 Rock* as CC a Democrat Politician, her performance parodies her life story, as much as it parodies the political world. However, rather than simply asking "What is it like to be a female prison manager?", "What is it like to live with a criminal husband?", "What is it like to be addicted to drugs?" or "What is it like to defend a murderer?", she makes us think in a wider sense: "How would you feel if you were the central character?" It is Edie Falco's ability to make us think about the complex issues that surround morality and the drive to be normal or good, in line with the pressures of what it is like to be vulnerable, responsible, guilty or compromised, that is central and non-judgemental. She however does not simply deliver a good performance, but rather presents a "nuanced" sense of self, in offering a sophisticated and engaging narrative rendition.

However as we shall see in the following chapter, storytelling is more complex in defining the heroic potential. The drive to be the hero or the heroine is not a simple destination, but rather a complex journey of humanity, where aspects of morality and the contexts of female identity unfold.

Notes

1. Edie Falco also appears in Woody Allen's *Bullets over Broadway* (1994); however this is in a minor role.
2. Father Phil is played by Paul Schulze, who also played Eddie (the pharmacist) in *Nurse Jackie*. Edie Falco and Schulze developed a friendship since working together in the film *Laws of Gravity* in 1992, leading to an enduring professional relationship.

4   The Heroine and Morality

Introduction

At the close of the pilot episode of *Nurse Jackie* (2009–15), we discover the extent of Jackie Peyton's duplicity that, while she is an exemplary health worker, besides being addicted to drugs, she is deceitful to her workplace colleagues, and more significantly is deceitful to her family. On returning home to her loving but oblivious family, in voiceover she states (within her internal monologue): "Make me good, but not now". In allusion to St Augustine's *Confessions* where the author expresses a desire to hold on to earthly pleasures, before giving of himself fully to the grace of God, *Nurse Jackie* references the struggle of the personal desiring self, and the challenge of striving for the common good, or the wholeness of self. *Nurse Jackie* frames the iconography of Catholic Saints, not only represented in the name of the actual hospital, All Saints, but explicitly employs the mise en scène of the chapel, where the statues of saints form a central focus, even after the chapel is formally deconsecrated by the diocese in season 3, episode 6 (see Figure 4.1). *Nurse Jackie* frames the struggle of the saint and sinner, in mediating the narrative of the addict attempting to find their way.

This chapter considers *Nurse Jackie's* representation of the seemingly immoral heroine, framing the iconography of the saint, or those working within the religious order. I argue that not only is *Nurse Jackie* a complex text, seeming part of quality television and the representation of the anti-heroine (Chapter 2), but its rendition of heroism integrates with a moral or virtuous imperative, more explicitly presented in mainstream film, which presents the struggle of "finding the right path", evident in films that represent nuns for example, such as in *Black Narcissus* (1947) and *Agnes of God* (1985). While these films might seem disparate to the generic form of *Nurse Jackie* in their focus on religious workers, it is the emphasis on spiritual heroism which is central, evident in psychological healing, as much as bodily healing.

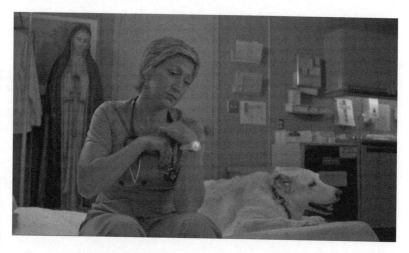

Figure 4.1 Edie Falco as Jackie Peyton in *Nurse Jackie*, series 3, episode 6, including the representation of a saint's statue (left) that was taken from the chapel, and a patient's dog.

Showtime, screenshot.

Hence the narrative drive of *Nurse Jackie* is for Jackie to be healed as a drug addict, as much as for her to heal any of her patients. The struggle of the individual is central, who is attempting to find their way, but is prone to the human condition, exhibiting weaknesses, desires, diversions and satiations. Central within this are the key notions of morality and heroism, alongside the notion of following, or finding a path.

Finding the Right Path and the Moral Imaginary

While Heidi Schlumpf (2016) writing in *The Catholic News Reporter*, and Kristyn Gorton (2016) writing in *Critical Studies in Television* have both theorised the meaning of *Nurse Jackie* with regards to the notion of "Saint or Sinner", with the former adopting a theological stance and the latter adopting a feminist critical approach, both texts frame Jackie's ability to do good, or care for people. Whilst these approaches are entirely valid, as inevitably in ethical terms to be truly virtuous within society, one has to care for others, I argue that *Nurse Jackie* is more complex in its mediation of the saint or sinner dichotomy. Most significantly when the character of Jackie Peyton asks that she "can be good", but suspends this notion, with "but not now", she accepts that she is unable to be good, in the moment of the present, admitting that she is human. Although inevitably Jackie is good at being a nurse, as clearly she is an exemplar and a role model to others, for example to Zoey (seeming as a mentor), there is no expectation that she wants to be good, but rather she is looking for some type of arrival. This arrival I argue is less about good deeds, and more about being true to her self, or achieving a sense of self value. I argue that central within this is not the achievement of some better way of being, but rather fully acknowledging her humanity, and her value to herself.

For example Jackie's addiction rehab sponsor, Antoinette, confronts Jackie after it appears that she is using again (Season 6, Ep. 7). Antoinette not only humorously remonstrates that "you can't fire me I'm still your sponsor", but also recalls a personal story, where at the height of her addiction whilst driving her car under the influence of alcohol her husband died as a consequence, and this was her lowest point. The importance of self is evident where she states:

> Wake the fuck up Jackie, for yourself. You can fool your kids. You can fool Frank, but you ain't fooling me. . . . When you hit rock bottom, I'm going to be there for you, because you're right, part of this is about me. I'm not giving up.

Central within this is not so much the need to hit "rock bottom" to find your way back, but that Antoinette admits that Jackie's salvation is part of her own need to move foreword. She admits to Jackie that her life story is entwined with that of Jackie. In other words her continuity of sobriety depends on maintaining a sense of personal worth, for herself.

A focus on self worth, or knowledge of self, is central in mediating the meaning of *Nurse Jackie* and the concept of being good. This I argue relates to Tim Dant's (2012) discussion of morality on television, which extends from the self. Dant tells us:

> Rather than think of morality as a system of ideas that are coherent and connected, as happens in the religions and ethical codes, I want to develop the idea of a "moral imaginary" as something more fluid and inclusive. . . . Instead of absolute values, the moral imaginary includes the complexity of feelings, relationships and extenuating or ameliorating circumstances that allow actions to be judged in terms of a specific situation.
>
> (p. 5)

The representation of Jackie Peyton as a complex character clearly involves moral judgements as to the consequences of her actions, and as to the instinct that drives her actions. For example depending on your theoretical analysis of virtue or moral philosophy, Jackie Peyton could be considered as related to "duty-based notions" or alternately "consequentialist notions".

In broad terms following Emanuel Kant's (1933) duty-based notions of virtue, motives for actions are central in mediating moral worth, framing a sense of duty relative to maxims. For example this would prioritise the maxim, "always help those in need, because it's your duty to so" over the maxim "always help those in need when you experience a feeling of compassion" (Warburton 1992, p. 41). In this way motives to do the common good irrespective of your own feelings in gaining something are central. This is hard to assess with regards to the character of Jackie Peyton, as clearly we see very strong evidence that she does often compromise her own sense of self or satisfaction in doing good deeds. For example, when Jackie Peyton delays her plans for escape (Season 6, Ep. 12) by aiding a car crash victim (see Chapter 1), even though she delays her journey which makes her vulnerable to discovery of capture and trial for fraud, we cannot be certain of her motives for action. Although it appears that this is duty centred, it is possible to argue that she may have done this good deed for her own advantage, to appear as the resolute professional, who might receive a lighter sentence if she were caught. In other words her maxim may be "always help a person if it maintains your professional identity", seeming non virtuous but actually self-serving, rather than "always help a person in need, irrespective of the danger to yourself".

However it is also possible to argue that the character of Jackie Peyton demonstrates a "consequentialist approach" within moral philosophy, following John Locke's notion of utilitarianism (see Colman 1983), that the greater good of society may be more important than the struggle or the trial of the individual. This is particularly evident in the pilot episode where, after the bike messenger dies; she falsifies an organ donor card, signing the name of the deceased person, in order that his organs may be used. Although this may appear as entirely unethical, she is thinking of the greater good of others, not necessarily herself. In presenting her internal monologue whilst signing the card, she affirms this, by saying out loud to herself: "you should have not died in vain". This seems clearly apparent, but we may also consider that she may experience some sense of personal worth in making this happen that could be about her ego, and an affirmation of power over life.

Despite this, it is also possible to argue that Jackie Peyton might be an exemplar of virtue ethics. As Peter Baron (2016) tells us:

> The key assumption is autonomy: we must be free to reason. To a utilitarian ethical norms arise out of the calculation of consequences, after we have accepted the happiness for pleasure is the only intrinsic good. But to a virtue ethicist norms can arise either out of a set of metaphysical

assumptions (when metaphysical means "beyond physics" or in essentially unprovable), or out of an observation about how groups work.

(p. 8)

I argue that Jackie Peyton is a virtue ethicist for her ability to suspend notions of the norm, modifying how she sees the world relative to her experience within social order. Also as Baron defines, "to be a virtue ethicist being honest doesn't necessarily include always telling the truth" (p. 9), and that realism is subjective, offering a critique of "other theories such as Kantian ethics and utilitarianism for failing to provide an adequate answer to the question 'why should I be moral'" (p. 9).

I argue that the moral integrity and potential of heroism within *Nurse Jackie* relates not so much to her deeds, but rather to her ability as a virtue ethicist. In doing this she attempts to find a way, or a path, in relation to her sense of self-identity as female. As Helen Jacey (2017) suggests a heroine's journey involves inclusivity, nurturing, intimacy, vulnerability and "reciprocity with others" (p. 100). However as Carol Pearson and Catherine Pope (1981) tell us:

> An exploration of the heroic journeys of women—and of men who are relatively powerless because of class or race [or sexuality]—makes clear that the archetypal hero masters the world by understanding it, not by dominating, controlling, or owning the world or other people. . . . Freeing the heroic journey from the limiting assumptions about appropriate female and male behaviour, then, is an important step in defining a truly human—and truly humane—pattern of heroic action.
>
> (pp. 4–5)

Hence the character of Jackie Peyton is an unusual heroic form. Although we might perceive her as a post feminist (Genz and Brabon 2018), evident in her failure to directly challenge male authority, and her acceptance of stereotypes which might surround her female identity as a nurse, her resolute strength is her ability to understand or comprehend, even if she makes mistakes. As Alison Horbury (2014) suggests, that while the rise of post feminism implies that heroine television dramatises an "erosion of second-wave feminist discourses [conversely] the methods deployed to comprehend heroine television have not similarly transitioned and 'feminism' acquires new cultural meaning in this space" (p. 219), offering potential feminist perspectives to diverse audiences able to understand the contexts.

Although Jackie Peyton is clearly an anti-heroine (Buonnanno 2017), her knowledge of self, related to imagined virtue and morality, frames her heroic potential. This I argue is less about "dominating, controlling, or owning the world or other people", but rather exhibits the potential to "understand" the notion of the self or the individual.

As a drug addict Jackie Peyton offers a complex prospect in defining the notion of the hero, as her heroic achievements might involve a deeper understanding of the psychology of the addict. Rather than transforming into a non-addict, or saving the world as an addict who must pay the ultimate cost (death), her heroism potentially extends from her ability to challenge myths within society concerning the value or context of the addict. As Carol Pearson and Catherine Pope (1981) affirm:

> Hero, by definition, departs from convention and thereby either implic- itly or explicitly challenges the myths that define the status quo. In doing so, the hero exposes the truth regarding society's distorted vision of the world and of the hero's own potential. The restrictive myths, which are potentially destructive forces, thus become a source of wisdom.
>
> (p. 16)

Such wisdom, I argue is evident where *Nurse Jackie* uses the myths that surround the addict to challenge or modify our understanding of the addict in society. However rather than simply inverting or parodying the myth, for example showing addicts as higher functioning individuals across the board (compared to non addicts), a sense of fluidity is presented in working through these ideas. Central within this is the ability to show the vulnerabil- ity of the addict in relation to personal experience. Within *Nurse Jackie*, this might involve the "technology of the self", in the exhibition of vulnerability, seeming as a kind of strength.

As Michel Foucault (1994) considers, relating notions of subjectivity within classical writing:

> The history of the "care" and the "techniques" of the self would thus be a way of doing the history of subjectivity; no longer, however, through divisions between the mad and the non-mad, sick and non-sick, delin- quents and non-delinquents, nor through the constitution of fields of scientific objectivity giving a place to living, speaking, labouring sub- ject; but, rather, through the putting in place, and the transformations in our culture, of "relations with oneself", with their technical armature of their knowledge effects.
>
> (p. 88)

Through framing the emergence of new forms of self-subjectivity where "the government of the self by oneself is in its articulation with relation to others" (p. 88), a fluid concept of the self emerges, not necessarily hindered by rigid social orders, or dominant narrative forms. In this context the self becomes central, rather than subordinate. For the character of Jackie Peyton, while she might be termed a female and not male, an addict and not sober, adulterer and not a devoted wife, and an absent mother (see Chapter 2) and not a "stay-at-home" mom, rather than as being termed as what she is not, her central notion of self is articulated within an emotional personally reflexive-based world, rather than an organised institutional-based world. As part of this as Geoff Danaher, Tony Schirato and Jenn Webb (2000) tell us: "one of the most important technologies of the self is self knowledge: 'knowing the self' involves determining the truth about the self, because only in knowing this truth can we work on ourselves to achieve perfectibility" (p. 129). In this way Jackie's pursuit to ultimately be good, even if it is not in the moment, reveals a technological process of working towards an imagined perfect version of self.

For example this may be evident in season 6 (Ep. 9); in what seems like a minor distracting narrative, the man who runs the candy kiosk dies suddenly. Very few workers in All Saints hospital ER department recall what the name of the proprietor actually was, as they were so busy getting on with their daily business. Only Jackie knows the full name of the manager, Naeem Reshamwala. This stimulates Zoey, who was ashamed for not knowing his name, to hold a memorial for Naeem in the chapel, with the attendance of many members from his family, alongside hospital workers. When individuals are asked to comment on memories of Naeem, only Jackie gets up and attempts to make a speech. However, after a few words, which seem entirely unlike Jackie (as she is usually confident), she is overwhelmed with emotion and is unable to finish. In this way, Jackie is presented as an earnest character, displaying a desire to work on herself for the good of community, even if she fails. However this brief moment is part of a larger narrative that concerns Jackie's search for self-knowledge, in attempting to understand the world, as a heroic character.

As Peter Sloterdijk (1989) tells us in interpreting the work of Fredrick Nietzsche and *Thus Spoke Zarathustra*:

> Through the act of leaving, the wanderer begins to discover what he has taken with him in spite of himself, just when he had thought he had left everything behind. The true self clings to the heels of the one who is embarking on the path. Only when one realises that he himself constitutes his own heaviest baggage can the "dialectic of the path" begin.
> (p. 33)

The representation of Jackie Peyton involves a journey of self-discovery in seeking the path to perfection or at least good behaviour. As Sloterdijk tells us a journey to self-discovery is complex, one that involves reflecting on your past, in attempting to move forwards. For the drug addict this is complex, as it is impossible to escape the identity as the addict. So in moving forwards, inevitably your shadow also moves forward with you, and moving ahead involves taking the past with you, reflecting on previous feelings and desires. Fluidity persists, in framing desires more than destinations.

Desire and Holy Order

For example consider the representations of nuns within *Black Narcissus* (1947) and *Agnes of God* (1985). In these texts notions of desire and tension between the body and the mind persist. As Maureen Sabibe (2013) tells us in her book *Veiled Desires: Intimate Portrayals of Nuns in Post War Anglo-American Film*, this engages with a wider scope in the representation of nuns on screen:

> These nuns enact the battle of the divided heart on-screen, torn by the conflict between their twentieth-century expectations as modern women and the traditional aspirations of religious life, and by the disparity between the Christian ideology of love expressed in agape and the emotional truth of the yearning desire known as eros.
>
> (p. 17)

For example within *Black Narcissus*, set in the Himalayas, as Ian Christie (1985) tells us:

> The temptations that beset the nuns and their insecure young leader, Sister Clodagh, spring as much from their own unresolved conflicts as from the ghosts of the windswept Palace of Mopu, where they have been sent to establish a new convent. . . . The English agent, Dean, treats the nuns with cool cynicism, fanning the flames of Sister Ruth's repressed desires. Clodagh keeps vigil over Ruth but cannot stop her desperate flight to throw herself at Dean's feet. In an extraordinary passage of vertiginous hysteria Ruth lies in wait for Clodagh as dawn breaks over the Himalayas, and tries to push her over the precipice.
>
> (cited in Butler 2015, p. 150)

Framing the repressed sexual desires of the nuns, leading to dramatic psychological and physical confrontations, establishes a female-oriented world where personal endurance and desires iterate the notion of self-discovery. This tension between bodily desires and the need to conform, or follow a noble path, is central. However failure or unimaginable desire is central (see

Butler 2015). Set in the Himalayas seeming as an exotic "Garden of Eden", the tension between the spiritual and physical world is framed, specifically apparent in the film trailer, where the voiceover attests, "They renounced the world of men, but found that the world was not to be denied". This reference is particularly applicable to Sister Ruth, who returns to the physical world of sexual desires, and is particularly apparent in her shedding her uniform as a nun, and then is seen wearing red lipstick.

In many ways *Nurse Jackie* is not that dissimilar to *Black Narcissus*, with regards to a subtext of desire, or physical satiation, which inhibits the imagined sense of moving forward. While the focus on prescription drug addiction is central within *Nurse Jackie*, and more conventionally within *Black Narcissus* it concerns the need to resist sexual temptation, the notion of the female heroic self that is defined through explaining the world rather than controlling the world is central. The female hero challenges male order, not so much through achieving a goal or building something new, but rather reveals a deeper understanding of human nature that allegedly can only be defined by the world of men.

However in *Agnes of God* the notion of desire is related to the fallibility of the body and the limits of comprehension with regards to childbirth. The film focuses on the representation of Sister Agnes, who is believed to have killed her new-born baby, but seems to have no knowledge of even bearing the child, let alone filicide. Agnes is subject to psychological analysis, where an investigation takes place headed by Martha Livingstone (played by Jane Fonda) that questions the authority of the Church, its belief systems and aspects of truthfulness. When Sister Agnes is under hypnosis, she recalls the birth of the child, and her discontent with God as the reason to murder the child, Agnes is revealed to be:

> The product of an abusive background [where she] lives in a world of faith, images and miracles. Although Martha [Livingstone] develops an acceptable hypothesis accounting for the baby's father, her hypnotizing of Agnes produces discrepant evidence and culminates in the film's ending, which leaves unclear not only the father's identity but also the fate of the film's characters.
>
> (Rasmussen and Downey 1989, p. 69)

Such a focus on uncertainty, not only with regard to the outcome of the narrative, but also with regards to the complicity of the religious order in protecting and/or abusing Agnes, frames the notion of vulnerability with regards to the physical body and the sanity of the mind. The screenwriters present a kind of virtue ethics based on individual experience, and the challenge to order, in challenging the meaning of the virtuous world. Central within this is the child that is seen as a product of shame, and the impossible role of the mother.

Hence both *Black Narcissus* and *Agnes of God* represent the life world of the nun within the religious order as vulnerable or subject to desire, framing the significance of childbirth and motherhood as something that is lost, or involving shame. The notion of the vulnerable body is central in forming a sense of virtue. For example in *Agnes of God*, Agnes under hypnosis displays stigmata (the sign of Christ having been on the cross, evident in bloodied hands) offering conflicting visions of Christ in relation to the nun, at the same time referencing the vulnerable child. A sense of lost motherhood is framed, whilst revealing the body to be vulnerable, as subject to desire.

The Nurse, the Nun and the Child

Nurse Jackie articulates the relationship between mother and child in a similar manner to *Black Narcissus* and *Agnes of God*. However rather than explicitly framing religious order, the notion of caring for the body is central in defining virtue. A heroic potential emerges, where the character of Jackie Peyton offers a deeper understanding of the world in framing her own failings as a reflective way of finding a path. In order to explore this further, I will examine Jackie Peyton's relationship to Paula (played by Judith Ivey) who is an elder retired nurse in season 1 (Ep. 6) in contrast to Helen (played by Dierdre O'Connell) who is an elder homeless nun in season 6 (Ep. 11). Both of these representations consider end-of-life narratives, but they also frame the life story of Jackie, relative to aspects of heroism, in offering a meaning of their lives. At the same time I will also explore the representation of Zoey, a junior nurse to Jackie, who appears as a surrogate child, and the representation of Grace who is Jackie's first-born child. These representations of children frame the goals or the reward that the character of Jackie Peyton perceives, in defining the meaning of her life, and her seeming failure to be virtuous.

The representation of Paula in season 1 and Helen in season 6, are in some senses similar. Paula was a nurse that used to work in All Saints Hospital, who is an old colleague of Jackie Peyton, but is now retired. She arrives at the ER department, unofficially, to get help to end her life, as she has terminal cancer. Helen in contrast is a retired nun, of a similar age to Paula. She is brought to the ER department as she is homeless, and has been attempting to end her life. Jackie offers support to both Paula and Helen.

In the case of Paula, Jackie argues with the management that she should be allowed to stay on the ER ward until a bed is ready in the oncology department. During this time Jackie surreptitiously creates a cocktail of drugs, in liquid form seeming like champagne, that she gives to Paula, at a time when many members of staff are gathered around her bed. Paula imbibes the fatal draft, and this ends her life peacefully. Although the staff gathered there do not openly discuss euthanasia, a sense of camaraderie is present, seeming like a "send off" to an old friend, who is leaving for a new job, or is about to retire. This representation frames Jackie's strength in making difficult decisions, ending the pain of a good friend. At the same time we get the impression that Paula's life story might be not that dissimilar to that of Jackie, that Jackie will end up lonely, and without a family, ultimately relying on a friendship network at work.

The representation of Helen almost mirrors that of Paula, in some senses bookending a sequence in Jackie's life story. Although Paula seems more like Jackie, as they are both nurses, in fact Jackie is more like Helen, as she is an (alcohol) addict. Significantly, Jackie identifies Helen's real trauma, and attempts to alleviate her alcohol withdrawal symptoms, by setting up an ethanol intravenous drip. Whilst Jackie had seen Paula as a workplace representation of herself, aware that she too might end up alone, Jackie sees Helen as an addict's representation of herself, aware that she might die in this way.

Jackie pays particular attention to the care of Helen, at one point personally washing her when Helen does not allow anyone else to do this. However Jackie takes advantage of Helen when Helen offers to help her in any way possible, in return for her kindness. Possibly seeing Helen as herself, and as such an unsalvageable prospect, Jackie asks Helen to pretend that her given name was Nancy Wood, the name that Jackie had used in falsifying an identity card, in order to obtain drugs illegally. Helen's admission that she was Nancy Wood potentially solves an on-going investigation that was closing in on Jackie.

However the manner in which Helen announces this lie, for the sake of Jackie, is significant. In a mirroring of Paula's death scene where many members of staff had gathered around her bed (discussed above), Jackie arranges something similar for Helen. In an allusion to Helen's former life as a nun (that she had renounced), Jackie gathers a number of female staff around her bed, and tells Helen, "these are all your sisters". However rather than what occurs in the culmination of Paula's life where she slips peacefully away, Helen shocks the gathered crowd by admitting to Jackie's crime, that she is Nancy Wood. Added to this when Helen eventually passes away, in fact she is alone, and only Zoey records her death. While this occurs Jackie is far away from the scene, high on drugs at the wedding of her former husband. This counterpointing frames Jackie's inability to face her own death, possibly from addiction, as occurs when Helen dies.

However the point of realisation is not so much our knowledge that Jackie had used Helen and she was absent for her death, but that Helen's death leads to a larger unravelling. The deaths of Paula and Helen, in different contexts, provide a mirror to Jackie's identity, reflecting on her virtuous potential. The former representing her workplace identity, and to some degree her relationship to addiction (or access to drugs), the latter representing her inner struggle with addiction, absence of responsibility and knowledge of her own impending demise. Such a "doppelganger" representation frames the changing moral universe that surrounds Jackie Peyton, between season 1 and season 6. While Jackie's care of Paula represented some heroic strength, through Jackie risking all to end the suffering of her dying old friend, Jackie's care of Helen seems more controversial. Despite this, Jackie's care of Helen did indeed consider her end-of-life plan that she was working towards. More significantly, a sense of camaraderie is evident when Helen contentedly lies to rescue Jackie from a criminal conviction. In some ways, Helen is respected as an equal to Jackie, as they both share a history of addiction. Whilst it is possible to suggest that the ultimate care of Helen was denied, as her life had more potential than Paula (who had terminal cancer), ultimately Jackie respected Helen's wishes, but revealed the complexity of ethical care.

Such a mediation of moral philosophy examining the virtue of relationships not only involves a focus on the sisterhood of nurses and/or nuns, but also involves a focus on the mother and child relationship. This is specifically evident in the representation of Zoey, who may be considered as Jackie Peyton's surrogate daughter.

This is particularly significant when Zoey confronts Jackie, after discovering the fake ID card amongst Helen's affects, which Jackie had created to offer false evidence that Helen was Nancy Wood, deflecting attention away from Jackie. Significant within this was the manner that Jackie had fraudulently created the ID card. When Jackie had washed Helen, and she was comfortable in bed, Zoey celebrated the transformation in Helen by taking a picture on her mobile phone. Jackie had not only used Helen, but also she had used Zoey, by asking her for a copy of Helen's image enabling her to produce the fraudulent card. Up to that to that point, Jackie had been like a mother to Zoey, an exemplar not only of good behaviour and professional practice within the workplace, but also an emotional source of inspiration and hope. This point of transformation offers a realisation that she will lose her surrogate daughter, seeming as a death of their relationship.

As Zoey states, when she confronts Jackie (Season 6, Ep. 12), referencing an earlier incident when Jackie had accidentally overdosed a patient with insulin:

Zoey: Oh, stop! Just fucking stop! Do you think this is about the insulin? Yes, this is about the fucking insulin. You used a picture of a dying nun to make a fake ID. . . . And then you convinced her—the very last thing she did on Earth—to lie for you and say that she was Nancy Wood and that she stole Carrie's D.E.A. number. . . . What's hard for me is you've been using [drugs] this whole time. . . . You stole a D.E.A. number. That's a federal offence. You can go to jail. If you don't go to rehab I will hand the picture over.

Jackie: Zoey, I—you have to believe me.

Zoey: I did believe you. I always believed you.

Through Zoey using the past tense "I always believed you", this signifies an ending of their trusting relationship. At the same time an inversion of roles takes place, where before Jackie had been the senior role model, and now Zoey is the more respected character.

Through representing Helen as a model for the ending of Jackie's life, and through relating Paula as a possible model for Jackie's elder years, it is significant that both of these mirror identities have no children themselves. They are both represented as childless and alone. This seems like the representations of nuns within *Black Narcissus* and *Agnes of God*, where similarly desire and potential motherhood are complicatedly aligned, and a sense of loss pervades. However in *Nurse Jackie*, the representation of Helen complicates the mother/child relationship. Jackie seems like a child to Helen, when she sensitively washes Helen in the shower room, in a manner that an older son or daughter might care for an older parent who is infirmed. Also Zoey acts like a metaphorical child to Helen, through taking a sentimental picture of her in bed, seeming more like a family photo than a record of a patient. Hence the notion of the child features as a key context in working through the heroic efforts of those involved in care, seeming to mimic the notion of the family in the manner that the nuns in *Black Narcissus* and *Agnes of God* might define sisterhood.

Despite this, the imagined failure of family informs our reading of *Nurse Jackie*, that crosses the divide between real families and given families, which might be based on kinship (Weston 1991) within workplace environments. Hence Jackie's relationship to Helen seeming as a metaphorical daughter, and to Zoey seeming as a metaphorical mother, inevitably is placed in context with her own real-life parent and child relationships. It is significant that Jackie Peyton, hardly ever mentions her parents, with the exception of an abstract reverence to her father in season 5 (Ep. 1) when she throws away flowers that he sent her on her birthday at work, suggesting that she has a poor relationship with him. She never mentions a mother, and consequently may be seen to be her own parent, to some degree explaining her self-sufficiency. Despite this, her relationships with her two daughters Grace and Fiona are complex. Notably Jackie's heroic identification with her daughter Grace signals her downfall, yet I argue frames her complex identity.

While Jackie loses what had almost been unconditional respect from her surrogate daughter Zoey after the death of Helen, it is ironic that during this time she believes that she has a closer relationship to her own daughter Grace. Since the outset of *Nurse Jackie*, we are aware that Jackie Peyton has had a difficult relationship with Grace. Not only do we hear that the child is depressed at school, including an incident where Jackie hears from her teachers that Grace fails to draw a picture of the family with a representation of the sun (Season 1, Ep. 4), but largely she is disturbed, preferring to watch documentaries of natural disasters rather than children's entertainment. As Grace becomes a teenager, she continues to be distant from Jackie, including rebellious and disrespectful behaviour, establishing their relationship as relatively toxic. However we find out in season 4 (Ep. 2) that in rehab Jackie had started taking drugs after giving birth to Grace (see also Chapter 2), stating:

> She's born, she starts crying, and she does not stop for two years. I'm holding her. I'm telling her everything's gonna be all right. And then you start thinking, "Does she know something I don't know?" She was just so, just so hurt, and by nothing. I stole 100 tabs of Percocet and never looked back.

Hence Jackie's failure to develop a valued maternal relationship with Grace is seen as the foundation of Jackie's addictive behaviour. Hence the goal of nurturing a better relationship with Grace is a central narrative drive for Jackie.

So it is significant that when she seems to make amends with Grace, in fact this contributes to her downfall. This however is connected to a turning point in her drive for sobriety. After Antoinette tells Jackie the heartbreaking story of her ultimate low point when her husband had been killed because of her addictive behaviour (discussed above), Jackie decides to allow Eddie, Frank and Antoinette to help her get off drugs. Staying at home, Jackie goes "cold turkey", with the aid of drugs supplied by Eddie to reduce the cravings. After a few days, Jackie seems to have battled with her addiction, and she appears on a sober path. Despite this, on the day that she seems to have recovered, Grace comes around to the family home, and confesses that she needs the love of her mother. Seemingly for the first time, Grace appears to want the love of her mother, looking for consolation, as a friend that she had fallen out with had shunned her at school, ironically over Grace failing to conceal a drug stash. However, a moment after the arrival of Grace, Jackie relapses, seeming to be triggered by the possibility that she could be a good mother after all. Her protection of Grace however is stimulated in acknowledging that Grace too is becoming an addict, and they share an impossible bond.

Just prior to Jackie's relapse at the close of the episode, when Grace returns, a brief exchange between Grace and Jackie, and then Jackie and Frank (who is aware of Grace's emerging drug problem), reveals the impossibility of the situation:

Grace:	I had a really, really bad day, Mommy.
Jackie:	Do you want to talk about it? . . . Can I make you some pancakes? In animal shapes? . . .
Frank [to Jackie]:	You need some help? . . . You know, look, the best time for her to be here?
Jackie:	She called me Mommy.
Frank:	I know, but it's a lot of stress, and Jack, they were her drugs. . . .
Jackie:	The only person in the world who can help her is me. . . .

Jackie immediately relapses after this exchange, seeming as if Grace were the drug that she cannot resist. Testifying that she is the only person that can help Grace offers an allusion to her identity as a drug addict, not just as a mother. This creates an impossible spectre for Frank, who suddenly realises that Jackie is as much an addict as a mother. While Frank also warns Jackie of the danger of helping Grace, admitting that he is not strong enough to go through another "cold turkey" session, a focus is placed on the impossible desire of Jackie to appear as the best mother as possible, in an allusion to "the making of pancakes" as fulfilling an idealistic family dream (see Chapter 2).

Hence Grace's sudden intervention, seemingly transformed as the ideal daughter, changes everything. Jackie regresses, and as a result her drug-taking momentum increases, leading to her abuse of Helen in attempting to conceal her earlier crimes. However this pathway is a human response to the impossibility of her relationship with Grace. In a similar form as represented in *Black Narcissus* and *Agnes of God*, in an idealistic world the notion of fulfilling physical desire and appropriately caring for a child seem like impossible prospects. In embarking on a quest to care for her child, in some senses following a quasi-religious path, Jackie denies her ability to be herself, but must address the shame that she feels for not achieving the ideal relationship with her daughter.

I argue however that her heroic potential comes not from this seemingly inappropriate path towards self-destruction, but is evident in her mediation of pain, as part of her "technology of self". Hence while Jackie does not always own up to her intents, such as admitting to Antoinette in season 6 (Ep. 10) that she had no intention of going to rehab, or that in taking the photo of Helen from Zoey that she would use it in a fraudulent way (discussed above), the audience get a glimpse of her conscience.

For example in season 7 (Ep. 1) when Jackie gets sober again, this occurs while she is briefly in a holding cell (discussed further below), under charge for possessing drugs when she was stopped by the police after aiding a car crash victim (Season 6, Ep. 12). Although later when she meets Zoey, she simply tells her that she was in rehab while she was away (not in prison), Zoey later finds out that this is a lie. Consequently Zoey takes an offer from the ER management to replace Jackie as Head Nurse, as she is unaware of Jackie's deeper regret. Jackie's regret is significant, as it frames a sense of conscience that seems like a rare moment of "truth".

This is apparent when Jackie was going through withdrawal in the prison without the support of medication. While she goes through this process in the company of other criminals held in the cell, Jackie stresses her regret in the way that she had deceived Zoey. Jackie experiences withdrawal symptoms, suggesting that this includes diarrhoea, vomiting and elevated temperature. She is represented as sitting at the edge of the cell, rocking back and forth, holding on to the cell bars, seeming like a caged animal (see Figure 4.2). In what could be considered a confessional scene, with an inmate listening to Jackie's confession, a frank exchange occurs:

Jackie: I feel like shit.
Inmate: Anything I can do? . . .
Jackie: You can talk. . . . Talk about, I don't know, why are you in here?
Inmate: Smoking weed on my stoop. . . . I'm just glad they didn't search my place or some shit because smoking pot's about the least illegal thing I do, you hear me?
Jackie: Yeah. [My crime is] DWI. And I've done worse. . . . Yeah, there's a young woman that works for me. She's kind of like a protégé, I guess.

In this brief exchange, Jackie admits her poor treatment of Zoey. With very few words, she states that this was serious, also framing the notion of a protégé. In an admission that in some way Zoey was a potential idealised version of herself, at her lowest moment of addiction withdrawal, we see a brief glimpse of her conscience, and her inner pain.

While Jackie does not expressly reveal this pain to Zoey, the audience are able to evaluate the relationship between the two characters, sensing a lack of conclusion or explicit comprehension. Hence Jackie's inner conscience seems contextual, and interrelated. This follows Bordwell's and Thompson's (1993) tension between the concepts of "perceptual subjectivity" and "mental subjectivity" (p. 78), where the former represents the explicit narrative

Figure 4.2 Edie Falco as Jackie Peyton in *Nurse Jackie*, series 7, episode 1, represented in prison as experiencing withdrawal symptoms, without the aid
of withdrawal medication.

Showtime, screenshot.

trajectory and the imagined subjectivity that is formed within the narrative,
and the latter relates the internal monologue that the character might express,
connected to their deeper psychology. The tension between how Jackie is
perceived and how Jackie perceives the world around her is fundamental to
our understanding of her heroic, self-reflective properties. Whilst Jackie may
be perceived as a poor mother who is addicted to drugs and is seen to fail at
everything, other than her ability to do her job as a nurse, she offers a vivid
representation of how we could understand the life world of the addict, as
someone inherently human in attempting to find their way.

Through her relationship with her "sisterhood", evident in her care in
providing "end of life" pathways for both Paula and Helen, and also her
care for Zoey, seeming like a younger sibling that she nourishes, Jackie
Peyton makes herself vulnerable through transgressing rules within her professional practice. This does not necessarily devalue her heroic potential, as
this is defined by her ability to understand the world, not necessarily control
it. While she seems like a failing mother to both Grace (her real daughter) and Zoey (her surrogate daughter), it is not the subjective perceptions
of Jackie that dominate—as drug user, as disloyal workplace colleague, as
reprehensible character—rather it is our understanding of her desire to take
a journey that might involve deep reflection and moments of earnest conscience, as much as transgress the rules that she is defined by.

Conclusion

In the final scene of *Nurse Jackie* in the finale episode of season 7 (Ep. 12), Jackie Peyton appears to pass away after overdosing on drugs, with her workplace colleagues around her, seeming to comfort her. Zoey cradles her head saying, "You're good Jackie. You're good". Kristyn Gorton (2016) suggests that this statement offers a moral closure, as Jackie has to be seen as inherently good, as a female character. Despite this, I argue that her relationship to the notion of the saint or the sinner is more complex. Jackie's heroic quality may be evident not in a final setting to terms, where she has to pay for her crimes, revealing that she is essentially good; it is apparent in her ability to be vulnerable.

If we consider the very final frame of the series, where workmates Zoey, Thor, Eddie and Dr Roman gather around Jackie Peyton's body (see Figure 4.3), a sense of Christian iconography is apparent, seeming like the disciples attending the body of Christ after taken from the cross. Viewed from above Jackie is represented as prostrate on the floor seeming like a Christ figure, with her attendants holding on to her body, in some ways not that dissimilar to the Italian renaissance painting *The Dead Christ Mourned—the Three Maries* (1603) by Annibale Carracci. The belief exhibited by those attending Jackie's body is that she was the core and heart of the ER Department.

Figure 4.3 Final scene *Nurse Jackie,* featuring (left to right) Betty Gilpin as Dr Roman, Merritt Weaver as Zoey, Edie Falco as Jackie Peyton, Stephen Wallem as Thor Lundgren, and (bottom centre) Paul Schulze as Eddie Walzer.

Showtime, screenshot.

Earlier in the final season we are aware that All Saints hospital has been sold, and this is the final day that any of them will work there. Jackie's demise is the demise of their shared universe. She appears like a Christ-like spiritual hero, in a reference to her leading a sisterhood, or a metaphorical family, in some senses referencing *Black Narcissus* and *Agnes of God*. However in the manner that *Black Narcissus* and *Agnes of God* represent a complex moral universe, Jackie's heroic quality is not easily defined.

I argue that Jackie Peyton represents a new form of hero that whilst might be termed as an anti-heroine (Buonnanno 2017), offers scope seeming as a technology of the self. We may consider that she is defined as either an addict or not an addict, or either a good mother or a bad mother, and equally either as a loyal colleague or a deceitful one; alternately we may define her as a complex site of reflection that encourages us to understand the addict's life. Whether she ends up good or bad is not the issue, even if the producers want to make it seem one way or another. Rather our understanding of Jackie Peyton is that she challenges: "assumptions [that] are embodied in myths, which oversimplify the nature of the social, physical, a metaphysical world and hide the truth about the heroes' identity" (Pearson and Pope 1981, p. 16). The character of Jackie Peyton is heroic as she attempts to find meaning, utilising her personal sense of virtue that she admits is often flawed.

When Jackie Peyton instantly relapses when confronted with the prospect of helping Grace, it is her heroic destruction of self, in seeming to follow the right path that dominates, rather than a sense that this is wrong. Tentative, ambiguous and even destructive moments as this define Jackie as the flawed hero, maybe someone that you cannot rely on, but inevitably an exemplar of the human condition, who is accessible to all.

As we shall see in the final chapter, such ambiguous heroic potential offers a rich source of identification, allowing audiences to experience a therapeutic potential that suspends value judgements, but reinforces the significance of the wounded individual, as a resource for all.

5 Therapy and Institution

Introduction

It is significant that the producers of *Nurse Jackie* (2009–15) represent the character of Jackie Peyton within a dream sequence just prior to her alleged demise. Wandering out of the fictional hospital of All Saints in New York, Jackie strolls through the streets ending up in "real-life" Times Square (see Figure 5.1). Witnessing a large community yoga session there (Solstice 2018), Jackie calmly wanders among the exercisers and sits down on the mat, as if taking part in the session. Jackie's serene representation as taking part in a yoga session frames the therapeutic nature of the series, at the same time juxtaposing her actual demise, as when she lies down we realise that this had been a dream, and in fact she is lying on the floor of the ER after taking a heroin overdose (discussed further below). The representation of therapy and the sense of physical healing or calming in close union with the emotional vision of passing away frames the meaning of the series. *Nurse Jackie* represents the addict's life, as part of contemporary narratives of therapy, woundedness and trauma.

This chapter consequently considers the narrative potential of *Nurse Jackie*, framing the significance of "therapy culture" (Furedi 2004) and "therapeutic discourse" (White 2002) within contemporary society. The series represents a new form of narrative that addresses new cultures of emotion, which suggest that caring and understanding potentially offer a therapeutic site of identification. At the same time, I argue that *Nurse Jackie* offers a critique of a neoliberal order, where the individual is represented as isolated and needing care. *Nurse Jackie* advocates social justice, where wealth is distributed fairly, everyone has access to welfare services, and is cared for with equality. This is evident where the series frames political healthcare issues in the Unites States, such as the advance of hospital closures, also questioning the suitability of drug rehabilitation programmes

Figure 5.1 Edie Falco as Jackie Peyton in the final episode of *Nurse Jackie*, in Times Square, New York.

Showtime, screenshot.

for nurses such as the Diversion programme (Darbo 2005). *Nurse Jackie* foregrounds therapy culture, whilst placing a focus on woundedness and responses to trauma.

Woundedness and Therapy Culture

The concept of the "wounded healer" is derived from psychoanalytical theory where a wounded individual helps others through sharing their "woundedness". As Carl Jung posited—"The doctor is effective only when he himself is affected. Only the wounded physician heals" (1989, p. 134). For example in a therapeutic relationship, the therapist's experience of alcohol abuse might in some ways foster a relationship, where a client senses that the therapist has been through a similar experience and is able to offer empathy and understanding. Within television drama the notion of the "wounded healer" often involves the representation of a "troubled" yet inspirational hero or heroine who seems like a role model but is a complex prospect. They are inspirational and active, yet often they are vulnerable and sometimes morally ambiguous.

The representation of Jackie Peyton as a "wounded healer" within *Nurse Jackie* seems to follow earlier representations, such as Gregory House in *House MD* (2004–12), Marcus Welby in *Marcus Welby MD* (1967–75),

Veronica Flanagan Callahan in *Mercy* (2009) and Martin Ellingham in *Doc Martin* (2004–), all of whom appear as physically and/or psychologically wounded. For example any character that has experienced a wounded past bears the potential to help others through understanding and empathy as a kind of role model, or exemplar of struggle for identity.

Such potential is representative of the wider concept of "therapy culture", which Frank Furedi defines as:

> The vocabulary of therapeutics no longer refers to unusual problems or exotic states of mind. Terms like stress, anxiety, addiction, compulsion, trauma, negative emotions, healing, syndrome, mid-life crisis or counselling refer to the normal episodes of daily life. They have also become part of our cultural imagination.
>
> (p. 1)

Furedi cites the example of the fictional character of the Mafia boss Tony Soprano in *The Sopranos*, who engages with a psychiatrist as part of this new representational world. Largely this involves a new focus on the importance of the "emotional script", relating the narrative significance of therapy, offering the ability for self-reflection. Central within this is a shift in how personal identity is mediated, relying less on traditional and functional ideas of identity, and more on personal experience.

For example, Furedi explores the rise in the use of the term of "self-esteem" within popular culture, and how its meaning has changed. Citing a meteoric rise in the use of the term "self-esteem" in the British press, from relative absence in the early 1980s, but emerging in the late 1980s to prominence in the early 2000s, Furedi frames the changing meaning of the term "self-esteem" from independence and self-regulation, and towards a need for self-knowledge. This reveals a popular cultural and identity shift, iterating the desire and ability to share your ideas with the world, suggesting that identity is more fluid, rather than fixed. Therapeutic culture in this way provides a means to share narratives of the self, indicating issues of vulnerability, relative to self-healing.

Nurse Jackie is clearly an exemplar of woundedness and therapeutic culture in this way, as the titular character of Jackie Peyton as an addict seems vulnerable to relapse. At the same time, she is encouraged to take therapy herself by those attempting to direct her pathway to recovery, including health professionals managing her rehab (in season 4 and season 7) and her personal rehab sponsor Antoinette (in season 6). Such an interrelationship between vulnerability and the need for therapy within the series defines the character of Jackie Peyton as an icon of therapy culture, representing the problems of both vulnerability and isolation.

Whilst therapy culture in *Nurse Jackie* seem to highlight important issues surrounding addiction within society, at the same time therapy culture is indicative of "risk society" (Beck 1992) and "individualization" (Beck and Beck-Gernsheim (2002), which potentially are problematic, and inherently related to "neoliberal order" (Saad-Filho and Johnson 2005). As Furedi tells us:

> Today, western culture makes sense of the experience of social isolation through interpreting behaviour through the highly individualized idiom of therapeutic discourse. Our culture has fostered a climate where the internal world of the individual has become the site where problems of society are raised and where it is perceived they need to be resolved . . . since the self is defined through feelings, the state of emotion is often represented as the key determinant of both individual and collective behaviour. Social problems are frequently recast as individual ones that have no direct connection to the social realm.
>
> (pp. 24–25)

Hence even if we have the ability as an audience to understand the plight of the addict through the individualisation of the addict's experience, there is an over-reliance on the personal world of the addict, rather than the social political universe that might offer support or understanding. While we may seem to understand the dilemmas that surround Jackie Peyton, it is this focus on the individual experience that is problematic. Although the focus on therapy culture is provocative and powerful in a discursive sense, such a personal focus potentially fails to engage with wider ideological contexts and issues.

Therapeutic Discourse and Power Resistance

However therapy culture might involve sharing issues, rather than purely focusing on the problem of the individual. In *Nurse Jackie*, confessional representations offer therapeutic potential for audiences to engage with. This might not only be evident in considering the actual representations in the series itself, but also it is apparent in the documentary commentary from the producers. Notably the personal documentary reflections of Liz Brixius, Linda Wallem and Edie Falco, which are extra textual to the series, offer therapeutic discourse in defining the life of the addict, as all have discussed their prior experience as addicts.

As Mimi White (2002) defines, with regards to the potential of the television audience:

> an indeterminate group of people can move in and out of positions of confessor and interlocutor instead of sustaining a more stable exchange

between two people fixed in positions of patient and therapist. Television viewers may in turn identify with someone posing questions [or raising issues] or with any number of interlocutors, including one who provides some sort of response; they can exert authority, such as it is, or recognize its limitation.

(p. 316)

White suggests that confessional performances emulate the relationship between therapists and patients, offering increased opportunities for audience identification. As YouTube user "Linsaiin" (YouTube 2018c) responds in an emotional text entry to the finale of *Nurse Jackie*:

This scene always makes me fucking cry . . . my mother is a lot like Jackie, without the nursing profession. this gets me so hard every time. The [conversation] zoey had with her was something i had to have with my mom . . . and i'm afraid for her and what she'll do in her life. but i can't worry about her anymore. That being said, I can't help but cry at this. I related to both Zoey and Grace and this show really pulled my heart strings.

(YouTube 2018c)

Clearly "Linsaiin" identified with the therapeutic potential of the series, making connections with her own life. Identifying Jackie's relationship to her daughter Grace and her "surrogate" daughter Zoey, "Linsaiin" sees similarities to her own relationship with her mother, stimulating an emotional response.

Added to this an audience might identify more explicitly with a narrative of care, where one person identifies with another. For example in season 3 (Ep. 4 and 5) Jackie Peyton cares for a patient named Lou, a middle-aged out-of-work salesman who comes to ER after passing out in a lobby where he has an interview for a new job. It is implied that he can no longer afford his blood pressure medication. In ER we discover that he has a minor head trauma, and from the fall he has broken his glasses, which Jackie fixes using adhesive tape. Dr O'Hara, disregarding protocol, provides Lou with a year's worth of pills for his blood pressure condition, inspired by Jackie's rebellious behaviour, and Lou is discharged. Later Lou returns to ER, even worse for wear, seeming highly depressed, and possibly suicidal. Jackie takes Lou to another hospital department, hoping that they can offer him an immediate psych evaluation. The receptionist tells Jackie that this is not possible at such short notice, but Jackie promises to offer flu vaccinations for the receptionist's family free of charge if she can get an appointment for Lou right away. Lou gets the appointment (see Figure 5.2). Later Jackie buys a new pair of glasses for Lou.

Figure 5.2 Haneefah Wood as Candace De La Brix (left), Edie Falco as Jackie Peyton (centre) and Michael Cumpsty as Lou Babiak (right) in *Nurse Jackie*.
Showtime, screenshot.

The care exhibited by Jackie for Lou offers a powerful site of identification as therapeutic discourse. Jackie understands Lou's isolation, and she interacts with him in a humane and caring way that extends beyond the limits of regular healthcare. Narratives such as this potentially stimulate therapeutic discourse for an audience, offering witnesses to an emotional caring interaction between characters.

Despite this, it is possible to argue that a therapeutic discursive engagement is limited. For example whilst "Linsaiin" (discussed above) offers clear evidence of identifying with the narrative, and in this case did publish a response online (through YouTube), this is largely about self-reflection, in a personal sense, offering an individual perspective. Equally any identification with the representation of Jackie and Lou might be read as simply advocating best practice within healthcare, rather than offering an exemplary moment of humanity that we might all wish for.

As Frank Furedi (2004) tells us, in philosophising the problems of therapy culture:

> [Therapy culture's ascendency] was not so much the cause but the reflection of the changing form of subjectivity. However, therapeutics was not simply the beneficiary of the crisis of the modernist imagination, it also

contributed to this process by distracting people from engaging with wider social issues in favour of the inward turn to the self.

(p. 203)

Therapy culture is more discursive than ideological, complicating issues of power. For example, although *Nurse Jackie* is emotionally impacting, in order to effectively address large audiences, and hopefully change the life chances of the drug addict, it potentially fails to engage with larger structures in society, such as encouraging institutional change. This might involve a direct address to policies within healthcare that might stimulate a change in practice.

In this sense therapy culture exhibits a discursive potential, in the manner of Michel Foucault's (1998) notion of modern power, where he suggests that "power is not an institution, and not a structure; neither is it a certain strength we are endowed with; it is the name that one attributes to a complex strategical situation in a particular society" (p. 93), but as part of this it fails to coherently engage with normative institutional contexts, such as those that might define the social order. In the case of *Nurse Jackie* this might mean that therapy culture offers a powerful point of identification relating the life story of the addict, but it does not necessarily address ideological issues regarding the treatment of drug addicts, inherent in mental health or social care organisations.

However as Candice L. Shelby (2016) tells us, in order to understand addiction:

> This means that we can and must address addiction at many different levels of analysis, because there is no question of one "level" based "root" of addiction, no one way of understanding what causes it, how it feels, or how it can be treated.

(p. 7)

Whilst therapy culture might in some way seem like a distracting form of subjectivity, as it is based less on ideology but more on emotion, it does provide diverse perspectives, that whilst they might not be conclusive are philosophical and engaging. Therapy culture offers powerful resistance to the norms of dominant ideology, as it does not purely focus on "one way of understanding"; rather it defines action as a strategy of interactions that stimulate responses.

For example when an audience witnesses the relationship between Jackie Peyton and patient Lou (discussed above), our focus is not only drawn to Jackie's emotional capacity but also it is drawn to the ideological failure of institutions. Jackie helps Lou because institutions in society have abandoned him, such as those that provide physical and psychological healthcare or support in finding employment. This involves a resistant potential that stimulates action. As Foucault (1998) suggests, within discursive power there is a plurality of resistances "that are possible, necessary, improbable; others that are spontaneous" (p. 96) involving personal challenges to order. Although therapy culture might seem discursive, and relatively introspective, it also has the potential to stimulate identity resistance that challenges institutional power, and "games of truth" that define authority. For the representation of the drug addict this might ultimately mean framing the resistant influence of recovering drug addicts (such as Brixius, Wallem and Falco) in challenging institutional ideals. As Candice L. Shelby (2016) attests, we should consider wider and different levels of analysis that are resistant. Through these means, real-life engagements with histories of addiction, alongside the creativity of fictional storytelling, offer resistant opportunities that might frame the depth of trauma and woundedness in defining political needs.

I argue that the contributions of Liz Brixius, Linda Wallem and Edie Falco are central, in working on *Nurse Jackie* as ex addicts themselves, in stimulating new resistant politicised discourse, framing the significance of trauma and woundedness. Specifically, the narrative arc of the last season frames the dynamics of the addict in relation to institutional failings.

The Addict, Institutions and Witness

Notably as Clyde Phillips tells *The Hollywood Reporter* (2015) in considering the ultimate meaning of *Nurse Jackie* in the final season:

> And have compassion if someone near to you [is an addict and] has this disease, think of it as a disease. If it were cancer, you'd think of it as a disease and you'd be compassionate. . . . There's a heroin epidemic going on now.
>
> (Hollywood Reporter 2018)

Although Candace L. Shelby (2016) highlights the problematic nature of considering addiction as a disease in over-relying on a scientific model, it "has lessened the stigma and blame associated with addiction" (p. 3). As part of this it is clear that Clyde Phillips' motivation in supporting the disease model is entirely political in working towards the better treatment and respect of addicts.

Clearly the disease model seems to be apparent in *Nurse Jackie*, as throughout the series Jackie relapses a number of times that seem incoherent in terms of uncontrollable desire, suggesting a kind of pathology and irresistible chemical force. For example at the close of season 4, after a year sober, Jackie seems to be recovered, but she simply relapses in a utilitarian and seemingly ordered manner. Later in season 6, when she has struggled with a few days doing "cold turkey" including being ill and she seems better at the end, she immediately relapses after just completing the task (see Chapter 4). Then in her final relapse in season 7, after winning her case to get her job back as a nurse (discussed further below), she simply starts regularly taking drugs as soon as she has won her case. In all these instances, it seems as if there is an uncontrollable force that appears to defy issues of feeling good and self-esteem that might encourage one to stay off drugs.

At the same time *Nurse Jackie* frames the choice model. Although Candace L. Shelby (2016) tells us:

> The element tying together the various types of choice theory is rationality. Theorists here either attempt to explain how addicts can be rational in repeatedly choosing something that is harmful to them, or they try to explain how a rational being can consistently choose irrationality.
>
> (p. 4)

Nurse Jackie also appears to present a rationality relative to the compulsion of Jackie Peyton. For example, when Jackie relapses in season 4, this was clearly planned, as she kept an opiate drug in a ring box, and it appears that all along she was planning to go back on drugs. Equally when she relapses after the "cold turkey" instance in season 6, this appears rational, as the trigger for this seems to be her need to help her daughter Grace, who believes that she can help with her life experience as a drug addict (see Chapter 4). Finally, when Jackie relapses in season 7 after winning her appeal, she appears entirely rational in waiting all this time to avoid detection so she can win the case. In this sense, Jackie Peyton can be read as both displaying the traits of the disease model, and the choice model.

Despite this in the final season (Season 7), it is clear that the tension between the models of disease and choice becomes more central, specifically with regards to the closure of All Saints Hospital, and the context of the Diversion drug rehabilitation programme, a scheme to get nurses back to work when they have had trouble with addiction (Darbo 2005). Hence although we may consider Jackie Peyton as an addict who is subject to the notions of "choice" or "disease", these are also inherent elements that could be applied to healthcare institutions, and their management. For example: how hospital management teams might be in some way "diseased" or make "inappropriate choices", possibly influenced by shareholders wanting to sell valuable assets in their failure to keep hospitals open. And might hospital management teams be in some way "diseased" or make "inappropriate choices" in their inability to effectively manage Diversion programmes possibly influenced by biased staff, who may consider the addict as unsalvageable?

In this way, I argue that the series frames institutional issues as much as personal issues, considering not only the trauma and woundedness of Jackie Peyton, but also the sense of collective trauma felt by individuals witnessing the actions of institutions. As Frances Guerin and Roger Hallas (2007) tell us:

> Trauma studies have sought to redeem the category of the real by connecting it to the traumatic historical event, which presents itself precisely as a representational limit, and even a challenge to the imagination itself. . . . Within the context of bearing witness, material images do not merely depict the historical world, they participate in its transformation.
>
> (pp. 3–4)

Hence I argue, following a trauma studies approach, that *Nurse Jackie* encourages audiences to share a collective sense of trauma. In witnessing the demise of the historical public service hospital, at the same time considering the institutional treatment of nurses working within these areas, a sense of collective trauma is presented that frames the culpability of institutions.

Hence the notions of "disease" and "choice" are not only reflected upon Jackie Peyton as a drug addict, but also these traits are applied to hospital shareholder/management teams, encouraging audiences to witness aspects of failure, demise and poor treatment inherent within them. The audience share a collective sense of trauma, in responding to the failings of institutions. For example, in *Nurse Jackie* we are aware that the shareholders are keen to sell All Saints Hospital for the sake of profit, rather than for the concern of the local community. Such a representation in fact references contemporary trends in the United States, where much-needed hospitals seem to be closing, and communities are losing valuable services.

While All Saints Hospital is a fictional site, it is significant to note that in many ways the real life Saint Vincent's Hospital in New York could be a model for this. Founded in 1849 and similarly following a Roman Catholic tradition, the hospital was sold off for luxury condominiums in 2010 (Hartocollis 2018; Hughesoct 2018), at the time the second season of *Nurse Jackie* was in production. While Saint Vincent's hospital ultimately filed for bankruptcy, it was similarly valued in the manner that the fictional All Saints Hospital is represented. As Joseph Berger reports, writing in the *New York Times* of the loss of Saint Vincent's:

> St. Vincent's, 160 years old and one of the major institutions of Greenwich Village, brought thousands of people to this sector of the

neighbourhood. Its 400 beds brought in not only patients but also their visiting families and friends. [Its] work force [had] included more than 3,500 doctors, nurses, administrators and others. . . . Naturally, many residents fret about the loss of nearby medical care.

Framing the significance of its historical meaning, in relation to the community setting and the reliance of local people, the loss of Saint Vincent's appears to be represented in *Nurse Jackie*.

Notably as, Mitch Smith and Abby Goodnough (2015) report, hospital closures are an increasing trend in the United States. Focusing on the closure of Mercy Hospital Independence in Kansas, they report:

> Mercy will be the 58th rural hospital to close in the United States since 2010 . . . and many more could soon join the list because of declining reimbursements, growing regulatory burdens and shrinking rural populations that result in an older, sicker pool of patients. Whether in Yadkinville, N.C.; Douglas, Ariz.; or Fulton, Ky., all of whose hospitals were also shuttered this year, these institutions are often mainstays of small communities, providing not just close-to-home care but also jobs and economic stability.

Seeming to come "out of the blue", recent hospital closures have affected local communities in an adverse way. Mercy Hospital Independence and St. Vincent's, like the fictional All Saints Hospital in *Nurse Jackie*, are seen as longstanding service providers to the community, that similarly had historical connections to the Roman Catholic Church. As part of this, a sense of "losing the soul" of the hospital is apparent, vividly explicit in *Nurse Jackie*, where in the final stages of its closure, the chapel that had been the "contemplative social space" of the series, and by token the hospital, is abused and destroyed. This is apparent when the Norwegian developer who leads the hospital's sale and its conversion to condos requisitions the chapel as a personal office.

At the same time, the suitability of the management team to supervise Jackie Peyton whilst she is under Diversion is questioned. As Nancy Darbro reports (2005), within professional healthcare environments: "a culture of stigma and mistreatment of addicts and alcoholics [may be exhibited] by many professionals" (p. 169). Hence when healthcare professionals as recovering addicts take part in the Diversion programme, not only must they work in a reduced capacity and are monitored by peers and management which may be humiliating, but also as addicts, they are subject to wider stigma and mistreatment inherent in the institution.

However despite these pressures, as Darbro reports, the motivation for individuals to embark on the Diversion programme involves a commitment to the nursing profession, she reports:

> The completers [of the Diversion programme] all reported that a primary motivation for them in staying in recovery and in compliance was the desire to keep their nursing licenses intact. They were committed to nursing as a career and would do anything to maintain their identity as nurses.
>
> (p. 173)

Following Jackie Peyton's statement "But if I'm not a nurse I'm no one" (Season 6, Ep. 12), individuals are willing to go through Diversion, as they are devoted to their professional identity as nurses. However, the treatment by management and peers can be oppressive. In *Nurse Jackie*, this is apparent when Gloria Akalitis, the manager of the ER department, considers that addicts are unsalvageable, relating her own experiences with her son (who is an addict) in relation to how she treats Jackie. This narrative element becomes apparent in the arbitration and appeal session (Season 7, Ep. 10), where Jackie's lawyer uses information of Akalitis's prejudice in arguing why the management is biased.

Hence *Nurse Jackie* encourages the audience to share a collective sense of trauma, in witnessing the management as bearing similar signs as those of the addict, such as making inappropriate choices, and seeming "diseased" in a sense. Through management seeming to over identify with personal bias, corporate profits and returns to shareholders, they seem to be failing the community. Hence notions of trauma are presented in *Nurse Jackie*, not only with regards to the experience of the drug addict, but also in eliciting the institutional failure of healthcare management, framing a collective sense of trauma. As part of this *Nurse Jackie* counterpoints the failings of institutions, while iterating the life story of the addict in regards to woundedness and healing.

Healing, Woundedness and Trauma

Darbro tells us relating the work of Valliant (1998), that an addict's healing and recovery might be related to key markers:

> (1) it occurs over the long term in terms of years, not months; (2) it occurs in a community environment or structure; (3) it is supported by compulsory supervisor and the application of consistent negative consequences related to drug use; (4) it is supported by engaging in a substitute, positive dependency that competes with substance use;

(5) it results from developing a guilt free and drug free social network; and (6) it involves membership in an inspirational self-help group.

(p. 180)

Illuminating key aspects such as time, community, structure, substitutes and resilience to resist guilt as much as drugs, recovery also might be stimulated by "pivotal events" in order for the addict to change their addictive patterns. Most significant within this is the alleged need to "hit rock bottom" (to feel the extreme depth of psychological stress or depravity) before an addict can realise that they need to change their behaviour. Despite this, Darbro reports that often in the case of nurses, a "pivotal event" might be stimulated by being caught at work, rather than feeling that they had reached an impacting psychological state. *Nurse Jackie* creatively provides the tension between fearing discovery, and likely experience of abject psychological depth in mediating the trauma and woundedness of the addict.

For example, within season 3, Jackie Peyton's marriage to Kevin begins to unravel. This is particularly complicated when Eddie (the ER pharmacist) makes friends with Kevin, as a kind of revenge for Jackie hiding the fact that she was married all the time while he and Jackie had a sexual relationship at work, involving his supply of drugs to her. In season 3 Jackie experiences a tension, not only that her husband might discover her identity as a drug addict, but also that her workplace colleagues might find out. Whilst in this season her best friend at work, Dr O'Hara, increasingly discovers Jackie's double life as an addict, and there are complicated tensions between Eddie, Jackie and Kevin that might lead the audience to consider that her secret life will be exposed, the notion of "hitting rock bottom" seems to gather momentum. Specifically, this is signalled when Jackie increasingly relies on drug dealer Bill, from whom she had initially stolen drugs when he was taken ill on the streets and Jackie came to his aid (Season 2, Ep. 10).

In season 3 (Ep. 3) a provocative exchange occurs between Jackie and Bill in a local diner after he returns to ER seeming to want retribution for her stealing his drugs. Bill tells her that he used to be a drug counsellor (see Figure 5.3):

> I burned out watching people relapse after getting sober too soon, so I decided to specialize. I'm the guy who helps people bottom out, find their all-time low by supplying them with drugs and then supervising their downward spiral for a hefty price. . . . I take people right to the edge till they beg for sobriety. I trawl the rooms looking for the weakest pie-eyed newbies with 30, 60, 90 days of sobriety, wait for them to relapse and then I make my move. . . . What I'm saying is if you need my help, I'll be around. . . . I've dealt with addicts for 20 years. . . . You took drugs off a man having an epileptic seizure. New low. Well done.

Figure 5.3 Edie Falco as Jackie Peyton and Bill Sage as Bill in series 3 of *Nurse Jackie*.

Showtime, screenshot.

In a very uncomfortable exchange, Jackie comments that his actions are "repulsive", but enquires if he thinks that she had descended low enough (in taking drugs off him as an epileptic patient), to which he responds "not even close". However Jackie increasingly meets Bill in order to obtain drugs (as she has become less close to Eddie, who was supplying her drugs), and in some sense in wanting to hit "rock bottom". At the same time, Bill appears to be coded as the devil, as later in season 3 (Ep. 6) Grace is investigating the lives of saints for an upcoming pageant at school, at one point consider-ing the fallen angel Lucifer. This is significant, as Bill seems to be tempting Jackie to risk her life, seeming to offer a perverse way to heal her, framing aspects of the supernatural.

In a pivotal episode (Season 3, Ep. 8) it is imagined that Jackie might reach "rock bottom" when she arranges to meet Bill at his apartment in order to obtain drugs. Jackie perceived this as unusual, as prior to this they had consistently met at a public diner, where they surreptitiously exchanged money for drugs. Earlier in the episode Jackie's daughter Grace rehearses for the school pageant, now deciding to play the role of St Christina. While rehearsing the life of St Christina, Grace is unsettled and disturbed, and there is intimation that she will be equally psychologically distressed when she does the performance later in that day.

It is now evening and it is dark, and Jackie is outside Bill's apartment block across the street, waiting to go in to get the drugs. As Bill exits the apartment catching Jackie's eye, we see a black bird land on a gargoyle from the high edifice of the building, which tumbles to the street crashing below, narrowly missing Bill. He looks down at the rubble briefly distracted from the traffic, and in an instant a large lorry swiftly runs him down at high speed, without stopping. The bird that had seemingly dislodged the gargoyle now lands on Bill's body, seeming like the devil now claiming his soul. Jackie looks shocked, if not traumatised. She briefly glances at Bill's prostrate decimated bloodied body like a guilty bystander from across the street, then instantly walks off.

After this we see Grace (played by Ruby Jerins) at the school pageant, where she is part way through her performance. She is represented on stage dressed as St Christina, in the costume that Jackie had made for her. The scenery depicts angels, and offers a gothic medieval vision. Grace initially starts her performance well, but then realises her mother is not in the audience and becomes distracted. However, in the far distance at the back of the theatre, Jackie emerges like a ghost from within the shadows. Grace sees her, then appears content and continues, acting more confidently articulating her arms:

Grace: I am the patron saint of insanity and lunatics. I died but came back to life. Psalm 102 is attributed to me. It is the prayer of the afflicted.

The camera then focuses solely on Jackie—as if looking down then closing more squarely on her expression—as she reflects on Grace's speech. Grace then continues reciting extracts from Psalm 102:

Grace: "For my days vanish like smoke. I am like an owl in the desert, among the ruins. I have mingled my drink with weeping, and my days are like a shadow. Pray for me".

It is what seems like might be the lowest point for Jackie Peyton, as she witnesses her daughter take part in the school pageant, all the while in the knowledge that earlier she had abandoned Bill who was gruesomely killed by the truck. Bill's death seems to have provided Jackie with the ultimate "rock bottom". Despite this our focus is on the meaning of Grace's performance that St Christina is the saint of the insane and the afflicted, and both Jackie and Grace are equally wounded.

A sense of an inalienable woundedness pervades, framing the almost incomprehensible life of the addict, involving culpability, shame, deceit and abandonment. At the same time a sense of ghostliness pervades, as Jackie seems to exist between the world of the living, and that of the dead.

While the episode closes with this ghostly vision, it is significant that this is not a finale, nor the ending of a series. This is purely an intermediate narrative within the series. Jackie seems to move on, more concerned that she has lost a supplier of her drugs than for her sense of personal value, or the road to recovery. In this sense, she buries the deep feeling of woundedness, but this movement was an explicit moment that frames her vulnerability.

Jackie continues as a strong character that whilst she may not be healed, exhibits a sense of personal resolve. At the same time the depths of Jackie's feelings pervade, all the while framing the failing of institutional bodies that underestimate or abandon her. Nowhere is this more apparent than in the final season, where a sense of Jackie's woundedness seems to overload, in many ways reflecting on the closure of the hospital.

The Nurse and the Hospital

May et al. (1985), advise us that:

> Woundedness is seen not as evidence of vulnerability but as the mark of knowledge . . . the wound validates the healer's ability to move "between the worlds"—the world of the well and the world of the ill, for it is in the bridging of these worlds that the healing power lies.
>
> (p. 84)

In the final season of *Nurse Jackie*, the sense of bridging worlds together seems to come apart. Jackie's wounded insight that in many ways brought people together seems to disappear, and the sense of woundedness that now pervades involves a focus on the isolated wounded individuals that surround her.

For example, while she had been wounded as an individual throughout the series, she had an ability to reflect on this pain, guilt or shame, and use it creatively to deflect attention, or to understand another's pain. Without the concealment of her pain, the diverse worlds unite, and the wound is contagious or it spreads without control. Hence when Jackie is found out, her attempts at control are rootless, because she cannot reflect on her strength in managing the wound. Her coping mechanisms change, from an isolated but powerful sense of inner strength, to a diffused sense of coping with others that relies on confrontation. An inherent and abject sense of loss emerges that is over-reliant on an interaction with others. Hence within the final season, in order to cope, Jackie's identity becomes fused to that of All Saint's Hospital.

Season 7 marks the end of All Saints Hospital, with its impending conversion into luxury condos. In close alignment the destiny of the hospital is unified with that of Jackie Peyton, seeming to bond the two as one entity. Although we only find out that the hospital is being sold to Norwegian developers in episode 3, it is significant that Jackie appears, at the outset, to head a movement to save the hospital, in a sense trying to save herself. Earlier in the series Jackie had fought a case against the hospital management to be reinstated as a nurse, as at the close of season 6 she had absconded, fearful of being caught for identity fraud to obtain drugs (see Chapter 1). Although at the outset of season 7 she goes to prison, her employers are just aware that she has been taking drugs again, and she eventually wins a case against her employers to gain a place on "Diversion", a scheme for nurses to go back to work under supervision to stay off drugs (as discussed above).

Jackie's woundedness is central, not only evident during her period under Diversion where she cannot have close contact with patients, seeming to lose her identity, but also it is apparent where she wounds herself further, after going back on drugs after winning her case to fully return to work. The dramatic sense of woundedness that was briefly made vivid to her after witnessing the death of Bill (where she reflects on Grace's and her own psychological state), seems to come to life in the final season. While the series had largely framed Jackie Peyton's wounded potential as a relative asset, in the final series, her wound opens up in relation to others.

Significantly the characters of Dr Prince (a new colleague, who shares Jackie's irreverence for authority), Zoey (her surrogate daughter, and acolyte), Akalitis (her longstanding ER boss, and colleague), O'Hara (her best friend) and Eddie (her lover), are represented as wounded characters in counterpoint to Jackie. Dr Prince is dying of a terminal illness and cannot help abandoning Jackie. Zoey needs to let go of Jackie, attempting to find a new life away from her. Gloria Akalitis cannot forgive Jackie for making her appeal to return to work personal, by accusing Akalitis of bias, in having a son as an addict that she cannot seem to forgive. O'Hara briefly returns to the series, but finds out that Jackie is using again, and cannot seem to forgive her. Eddie is willing to go to prison for Jackie, taking full responsibility for a crime they both committed where they sold his sales rep sample drugs to a "pill mill" (a pretend medical centre, that is in fact a place to buy illegal drugs). All of these characters, with the exception of Dr Prince and Eddie, ultimately cannot accept her identity as a drug addict. Their own perceived actions involve aspects of self-protection, in some ways moving on without Jackie. While Dr Prince and Eddie accept Jackie as she is, both relationships seem to lack a future, as Dr Prince will shortly pass away, and Eddie is heading for prison. These events lead Jackie to over medicate herself, taking a heroin overdose using hard core drugs left by an ER patient, which leads to her death.

However, we should remember that Jackie represents the hospital as much as the drug addict. Jackie is the final patient that cannot be saved. A sense of "no future" pervades, for both the community and for Jackie. Jackie like the hospital is wounded, beyond repair. When the doors are finally closed to the ER department at All Saints, which had not been shut for "centuries", there is a sense of an ending. Like the real-life hospital of St Vincent's that closed while the series was in production, a community resonance is evident, that frames this idea of a lost world, as much as a loss to the individual. Behind the closed doors to the ER room lies an isolated space that seems to have lost its meaning. Jackie's overdose on heroin is a cultural, as much as a psychological, response to failure.

Nurse Jackie frames the woundedness of the drug addict and the woundedness of society that fails to protect itself or its own. While the wounded healer inevitably has insight, and can potentially heal, without a relative unconditional understanding of the self, or structures that may care, a sense of loss dominates. *Nurse Jackie* politicises the loss of understanding, as much as the loss of community resources. It is imagined that we have finally given up on Jackie Peyton, as she has gone beyond the limits of approval. However the closure of the hospital seems to envelop the narrative, as without community healthcare, people like Jackie cannot be cared for, or be employed.

Conclusion

However, Jackie Peyton's demise might be a beginning rather than an ending. In a dream sequence before her death, the juxtaposition of Times Square where Jackie takes part in a yoga session offers a direct reference to therapy culture and the opportunity to heal. At the same time, we are encouraged to understand Jackie's woundedness. When she witnesses the death of drug dealer Bill, she is represented as a helpless victim of her own actions, which includes an understanding of the psychological state of her daughter, Grace. The drive towards healing, but an acceptance of woundedness, offers prospects for recovery.

While we know that Jackie eventually seems to pass away, it is not so much the destination, but the journey that remains. The producers of *Nurse Jackie* take the audience on a journey that they know will ultimately end, but I argue that they are less concerned for the outcome of the story, or the punishment that she may receive, but rather focus on the experience of the pathway. As Candace L. Shelby (2016) tells us:

> Understood better as a process rather than as a state, addiction is essentially a temporal phenomenon, [which involves] addicts' wishes to avoid use and their plans for using are temporally distinct, [besides this] it takes time for human addiction to develop, and to dissipate.

(p. 2)

Time indeed informs our understanding of the addict's narrative, but is process based, rather than destination based. The strength of *Nurse Jackie* is that the producers understand the life of the addict, in which total recovery is unlikely, and that the addict's life is a work in progress.

However this process involves a focus on institutions that surround Jackie Peyton, as much as a representation of an addict's story. The loss of the fictional All Saints Hospital inspires us to consider real-life losses, such as the loss of Saint Vincent's Hospital in New York, the possible model for the setting of *Nurse Jackie*. The life world of Jackie Peyton is bound up with that of the hospital. More than a moral tale, but rather a complex world that intersects political issues of understanding and care, a focus is placed upon pressures in the workplace. As Kristyn Gorton (2016) suggests, the viewers of *Nurse Jackie* "are taken on an emotional journey through her character's addiction. They also [experience] Jackie's destructive behaviour, her rebellious approach and, ultimately, her failure to cope with the demands of a neo-liberal workplace" (p. 158). However, I would argue it is precisely her human condition in ultimately meeting the demands of the workplace, but challenging its authority, that is central.

As the doors of All Saints Hospital close, this suggests an impossible scenario for Jackie as much as it represents the loss of a caring community. Jackie Peyton is an idealised form of social agent; she may break the rules, she may hurt people, she may let people down, but ultimately she cares for the "un-named", the lost and the disenfranchised.

In the manner that Jackie cares for Lou in season 3 where she not only stimulates Dr O'Hara to provide him with free medication (for a year), but also she gets him urgent attention that he needs whilst depressed and replaces his broken glasses (discussed above), *Nurse Jackie* frames the heroic nature of the individual in the workplace, unlikely to be rewarded by management. Jackie's reward is our understanding of her kindness, at the same time accepting her human struggles in facing the burden of addiction. As an idealised, but flawed, social agent, inevitably the structures will break, as evidenced in the closing of All Saints Hospital itself. At the same time Jackie's "breaking" is not structural at all, but it is our reflection. We understand the failure of community, to care for all, but we are not innocent bystanders ourselves.

Conclusion
A Call to Action

When Evan Dunsky conceived the original idea of *Nurse Jackie* (2009–15) under the working title of *Nurse Mona*, he probably never imagined how the series would develop. Originally a metaphysical and relatively gothic concept that according to Liz Brixius and Linda Wallem involved elements of the supernatural and the paranormal (see Introduction), ultimately the birth of the series was a union of Dunsky, Brixius, Wallem and Edie Falco. While later (after season 4) Clyde Phillips would offer creative input as the new series show runner, ultimately the series has been collaborative. Hence the development of *Nurse Jackie*, much like the work ethic of Edie Falco herself, involves a team work principle, as much as a central ideological or authorial vision.

Despite this collaborative and team work ethic in producing and developing the series, it is also important to note both the context of Showtime itself, as a premium cable television producer, and Edie Falco, as an iconic actress who had starred in *The Sopranos* (1999–2007). In this way, the narrative and discursive development of the series is clearly important in its relationship to modes of production and distribution, and the emerging star persona of Falco is central. In this sense *Nurse Jackie* is a creative narrative text that owes much to the emergence of quality television and the history of *The Sopranos* and HBO, and the significance of celebrity and star persona.

Central within this has to be Edie Falco. Her acting performance involving her ability to connect to audiences is particularly significant. Most notably Falco's own history of addiction appears to be the key element that binds the series. Whilst she avoids any suggestion that she directs the series, not only does the character of Jackie Peyton seem to represent in some ways Falco's own life story and emotional universe, but also she was influential in the original casting of the show, and more significantly highly invested in defining the meaning of the series and its outcome. For example where Edie Falco discusses the final episode:

> I have very personal feelings about that stuff because of my own addiction, but also that of many people in my life who I love. It was important

to me, personally, that it be taken seriously as the epidemic that it is. I thought, "Well, look. If you guys have her doing drugs and not going to any kind of therapy or meetings or rehab with any consistency, this can't end well". Because that's not fair to the viewership, who may be watching and thinking, wait a second, that's not what happened to my family. I really wanted it to be . . . clear that she died at the end.

(Nevins 2018)

While Falco admits that there was a relative battle with the production team to agree to this outcome, leaving the series with an ambiguous ending where it is not entirely clear that Jackie has passed away, she states, "If you ask me, she died" (AAT 2018). Edie Falco's star presence ultimately defines the meaning of the series, at the same time building on her work within television and film.

Nurse Jackie is part of body trauma TV (Jacobs 2003) involving a history of prior medical dramas, such as *St. Elsewhere* (1982–88), *ER* (1994–2009) and *House MD* (2004–12), where the ensemble cast offer a sense of community, but the notion of the wounded healer is central. Also through framing the strong female in the New York workplace, *Nurse Jackie* clearly continues a tradition within television drama that involves foundational texts such as *Rhoda* (1974–78), *Cagney and Lacey* (1981–88), *NYPD Blue* (1993–2005) and *Sex and the City* 1998–2004). The notion of the female worker offers a creative prospect in questioning the contemporary shift to neoliberalism. *Nurse Jackie* offers insight into today's changing workplace environment, where not only is there less security in working for organisations, but also we are expected to outperform others to keep our jobs.

Within *Nurse Jackie*, the role of the nurse is related to "sisterhood", in many ways referencing the bond of nuns within a holy order. As part of this not only is the chapel in the fictional hospital of All Saints, a central point of contemplative energy, but also religion plays a key part in mediating the notion of healing. Specifically *Nurse Jackie* references the representation of nuns evident in films such as *Black Narcissus* (1947) and *Agnes of God* (1985), where human desire and emotions are complicated elements, both enabling and inhibiting a consistent moral universe. Frequently the saint and sinner dichotomy is presented, referencing both the potential to do good deeds, or to be true to oneself.

Nurse Jackie frames morality relative to the emotional world of soap opera and the notion of female heroism. With Jackie Peyton seeming in some ways as an anti-heroine, the series also offers a complex moral universe, where the life world of the addict is played out in sophisticated ways. With Jackie Peyton appearing to be a virtue ethicist, who in philosophical terms might suspend the notion of the norm in working out what is virtuous behaviour, a sense of realism is foregrounded. Her imagined care for people seems to be of the very highest standard, yet she is morally compromised through reflecting on her actions. At the same time she is a role model to others, even in contexts where her humanity and vulnerability make it difficult for her to do her job.

Nowhere could this be more apparent than in the involvement of scriptwriters Liz Brixius and Linda Wallem, who as ex addicts of prescription drugs themselves are the ultimate creators of the series, along with Evan Dunsky (discussed above). Their commitment to tell the story of prescription drug addiction offers a deep cultural resonance. Most significantly they tell the story of the opiate addiction epidemic, largely enabled through the remarketing of time-release painkillers, such as OxyContin. As Sam Quinones reports, this is an all-consuming story "about addiction and marketing, about wealth and poverty, about happiness and how to achieve it. [It is] an epic woven from threads from all over" (p. 8). Revealing the connectedness of society, and the inter reliance of individuals, Quinones reflects the impact on society that clearly Brixius, Wallem, Dunsky, Phillips and Edie Falco engage with.

The story of the opiate epidemic as told through *Nurse Jackie* not only involves a human and personal factor in exploring the life world of the addict, but also it contextualises the failings of institutions. In the manner that the real life closing of Saint Vincent's Hospital in New York might be the inspiration for the closure of the fictional All Saints Hospital in *Nurse Jackie*, the series frames the failing of society to care for all. As part of this *Nurse Jackie* is a call to action, involving a reflection on society's failings, more than those of the addict.

This call however is a complex prospect; *Nurse Jackie* is part of therapeutic culture, which seems introspective and contemplative, rather than extrovert and action oriented. The series opens up a discussion about how we might engage with the addict, at the same time framing the significance of the mother (Jackie Peyton) who might be absent, but is trying to find her way back. As we know, the representation of female identity, like representations of minority groups including those that surround race, ethnicity and sexuality, involves a focus on the periphery rather than the centre. Even if Jackie Peyton were to get off drugs, and if she thought that she had become a satisfactory mother, our cultural world would still define her as "outside". Outside as a recovering drug addict, and outside as a mother, she would remain on the periphery of representational power.

The current epidemic in opiate addiction involves many who are outside. Our task in reading *Nurse Jackie* should not be to desire some recovery, or some sense of an ending; it should be a call to action for all. In the manner that Edie Falco (see Figure 6.1) within the personal family history documentary *Who Do You Think You Are* (2012) states:

> I tend to believe that so much of family is about nurture. . . . It really clarified for me what family really means, which has very little to do

Figure 6.1 Edie Falco on board a galleon in *Who Do You Think You Are?*
NBC, screenshot.

with what country your great great great great grandfather lived in, and more about what emotional clouds you were surrounded in as you grew up. And that meant a great deal to me, it made me so much more solid about having adopted kids, and it really is more about the people who have loved you and cared for you.

Edie Falco in discussing her ancestors, some of whom were orphaned, subverts the narrative of *Who Do You Think You Are* by advising that family is formed not so much through blood relationships, but rather relates how we nurture or care for others, in the manner of Kath Weston's (1991) "families we choose".

Edie Falco's contribution to *Nurse Jackie* is personal, it is political and it is family oriented. She seems to advocate a call to action utilising her "autobiographical self" (Pullen 2016b), suggesting that we should better care for each other. She argues that we should define our notions of family and community, less based on the rules of engagement, but rather on how we are connected and how we need each other.

In the manner that Sam Quinones (2016) recalls the historical idealistic swimming pool environment in Portsmouth, Ohio, as representing an American Dream that is now lost, our task is not to recreate that historical and emotionally charged saturated past. It should be to define new ways of connecting. *Nurse Jackie* offers evidence that the American Dream is lost through the individual relying on opiates to make it through the day; at the same time it defines our relationship to others as not necessarily reliant on traditional family forms. We might not easily connect to the life of the addict, but we might better comprehend what it means to be human, vulnerable, isolated, abject and frail. In *Nurse Jackie* the American Dream and the addict's dream world are connected, offering scope to wake up and become aware as much to take action.

References

AAT. 2018. Archive of American Television: Edie Falco. www.emmytvlegends.org/interviews/people/edie-falco# [Accessed 12 February, 2018].

ABC. 2018. ABC Interview. http://abcnews.go.com/GMA/video/edie-falco-talks-upcoming-nurse-jackie-season-tv-23378535 [Accessed 31 January, 2018].

Akass, K. and McCabe, J. 2017. Adieu Carmela Soprano! Lessons from the HBO Mobster Wife on TV Female Agency and Neo-Liberal (Narrative) Power. In M. Buonanno (ed.) *Television Antiheroines: Women Behaving Badly in Crime and Prison Drama*. Bristol: Intellect, pp. 67–81.

Ang, I. 2007. Television Fictions around the World: Melodrama and Irony in Global Perspective. *Critical Studies in Television*, Vol. 2, No. 2, pp. 18–30.

Baron, P. 2016. *Virtue Ethics*. Wells: Peped.

Baruch. 2018. Newman Vertical Campus becomes all Saints Hospital for 'Nurse Jackie'. www.baruch.cuny.edu/news/nvcnursejackie09.htm [Accessed 12 February, 2018].

Beck, B. 2012. Mother Courage and Her Soaps: *Incendies, Weeds, Nurse Jackie*, and Daytime Drama. *Multicultural Perspectives*, Vol. 14, No. 1, pp. 28–31.

Beck, U. 1992. *Risk Society: Towards a New Modernity*. London: Sage.

Beck, U. and Beck-Gernsheim, E. 2002. *Individualization*. London: Sage.

Bordwell, D. and Thompson, K. 1993. *Film Art: An Introduction*. Fourth Edition. New York: McGraw-Hill.

Bowes, M. 1990. Only When I Laugh. In A. Goodman and G. Whannel (eds.) *Understanding Television*. London: Routledge, pp. 128–140.

Boynton, A. 2018. Remembering St' Vincent's. *New Yorker*, May 16, 2013. www.newyorker.com/culture/culture-desk/remembering-st-vincents [Accessed 12 February, 2018].

Brunsdon, C. 1997. *Screen Tastes: Soap Opera to Satellite Dishes*. London: Routledge.

Buonnanno, M. 2017. *Television Antiheroines: Women Behaving Badly in Crime and Prison Drama*. Bristol: Intellect.

Butler, B. 2018. Is There Anything You Can't Say on TV Anymore? It's Complicated. *Washington Post*, March 29, 2016. www.washingtonpost.com/news/arts-and-entertainment/wp/2016/03/29/is-there-anything-you-cant-say-on-tv-anymore-its-complicated/?utm_term=.8d5a683285b6 [Accessed 4 April, 2018].

Butler, D. 2015. Powell and Pressburger's Black Narcissus: A Study in Loneliness and Loss of the Soul. *Psychodynamic Practice*, Vol. 21, No. 2, pp. 147–159.

Christenson, P. G., Henriksen, L., Roberts, D. F., Kelley, M., Carbone, S. and Wilson, A. B. 2000. Substance Use in Popular Prime Time Television. https://permanent.access.gpo.gov/lps19217/supptt.pdf [Accessed 4 April, 2018].

Christie, I. 1985. *Arrows of Desire: The Films of Michael Powell and Emeric Pressburger*. London: Waterstone.

Colman, J. 1983. *John Locke's Moral Philosophy*. Edinburgh: Edinburgh University Press.

Creative Resistance. 2018. Latest Video: Lu Lu Land: Edie Falco Explains How the IDC Are Handing New York State to the Republicans. www.thecreativeresistance.us/#video-section [Accessed 10 February, 2018].

Cullen, J. 2003. *The American Dream: A Short History of an Idea That Shaped a Nation*. New York: Oxford University Press.

D'Acci, J. 1987. The Case of Cagney and Lacey. In H. Baehr and G. Dyer (eds.) *Boxed in: Women and Television*. London: Pandora Press, pp. 203–226.

Daily Kos. 2018. Edie Falco Explains Why Fake Dems Are Handling New York to Republicans in This Video. www.dailykos.com/stories/2017/10/25/1709797/-Edie-Falco-explains-how-fake-Dems-are-handing-New-York-to-Republicans-in-this-video [Accessed 12 February, 2018].

Danaher, G., Schirato, T. and Webb, J. eds. 2000. *Understanding Foucault*. London: Sage.

Dant, T. 2012. *Television and the Moral Imaginary: Society through The Small Screen*. Basingstoke: Palgrave MacMillan.

Darbo, N. 2005. Alternative Diversion Programs for Nurses with Impaired Practice: Completers and Non-Completers. *Journal of Addictions Nursing*, Vol. 16, pp. 169–185.

Dyer, R. 1986. *Heavenly Bodies: Film Stars and Society*. London: British Film Institute.

Dyer, R. 2001. *Stars*, rep. London: British Film Institute.

Edelman, L. 2004. *No Future: Queer Theory and the Death Drive*. Durham: Duke University Press.

Elliott, A. 1996. *Subject to Ourselves: Social Theory, Psychoanalysis and Postmodernity*. Cambridge: Polity Press.

FCC. 2018. www.fcc.gov/ [Accessed 12 February, 2018].

Foucault, M. 1994. *Ethics: Essential Works of Foucault 1954–1984*. Volume 1. London: Penguin.

Foucault, M. 1998. *The History of Sexuality*. Volume 1. London: Penguin.

Furedi, F. 2004. *Therapy Culture: Cultivating Vulnerability in an Uncertain Age*. London: Routledge.

Gabrielson, T. 2009. The End of New Beginnings: Nature and the American Dream in the *Sopranos, Weeds*, and *Lost. Theory and Event*, Vol. 12, No. 2.

Genz, S. and Brabon, B. 2018. *Postfeminism: Cultural Texts and Theories*. Edinburgh: Edinburgh University Press.

Geraghty, C. 1991. *Women and Soap Opera: A Study of Prime Time Soaps*. Cambridge: Polity Press.

Giddens, A. 1992. *Modernity and Self Identity: Self and Society in the Late Modern Age*, rep. Cambridge: Polity Press.

Gorton, K. 2016. 'Walking the Line between Saint and Sinner': Care and Nurse Jackie. *Critical Studies in Television: The International Journal of Television Studies*, Vol. 11, No. 2, pp. 151–163.

Guerin, F. and Hallas, R. 2007. *The Image and the Witness: Trauma, Memory and Visual Culture*. London: Wallflower Press.

Hall, S. 1997. The Spectacle of the 'Other'. In S. Hall (ed.) *Representation: Cultural Representations and Signifying Practices*. London: Sage, pp. 223–279.

Hall, S. 1998. The Going Nowhere Show. In A. Chadwick and R. Hefferman (eds.) *The New Labour Reader*. Cambridge: Polity Press.

Hartocollis, A. 2018. Bankrupt St. Vincent's Moves toward Selling Hospital Site, December 1, 2010. www.nytimes.com/2010/12/02/nyregion/02vincent.html [Accessed 12 February, 2018].

Harwood, S. 1997. *Family Fictions: Representations of the Family in 1980s Hollywood Cinema*. Basingstoke: Palgrave MacMillan.

Hirt, C., Wong, K., Erichsen, S. and White, J. S. 2013. Medical Dramas on Television: A Brief Guide for Educators. *Medical Teacher*, Vol. 35, pp. 237–242.

Hockley, L. and Gardner, L. eds. 2011. Introduction. In *House: The Wounded Healer on Television: Jungian and Post-Jungian Reflections*. London: Routledge, pp. 1–7.

Hollywood Reporter. 2018. www.hollywoodreporter.com/live-feed/nurse-jackie-series-finale-ending-787038 [Accessed 12 February, 2018].

Horbury, A. 2014. Post-Feminist Impasses in Popular Heroine Television. *Continuum: Journal of Media & Cultural Studies*, Vol. 28, No. 2, pp. 213–225.

Hughesoct, C. J. 2018. Where St. Vincent's Once Stood. October 25, 2013. www.nytimes.com/2013/10/27/realestate/where-st-vincents-once-stood.html [Accessed 15 February, 2018].

Jacey, H. 2017. *The Woman in the Story: Writing Memorable Female Characters*. Los Angeles: Michael Wise Productions.

Jacobs, J. 2003. *Body Trauma TV: The New Hospital Dramas*. London: British Film Institute Publishing.

Jameson, F. 1991. *Postmodernism or the Cultural Logic of Late Capitalism*. London: Verso.

Jones, N. 2018. Coffee with Edie Falco, Buddhist Mom of the West Village. 30 March. www.vulture.com/2018/03/edie-falco-interview.html [Accessed 24 April, 2018].

Jung, C. G. 1989. *Memories, Dreams, Reflections*. New York: Vintage Books.

Jung, C. G. 2002. *The Archetypes and the Collective Unconscious*. Second Edition. New York: Routledge.

Kant, E. 1933. *Critique of Pure Reason*. London: Palgrave MacMillan.

Kaplan, A. E. 1992. *Motherhood and Representation: The Mother in Popular Culture and Melodrama*. London: Routledge.

Kennedy, L. 2000. *Race and Urban Space in Contemporary American Culture*. Edinburgh: Edinburgh University Press.

Lotz, A. 2014. *Cable Guys: Television and Masculinities in the 21st Century*. New York: New York University Press.

Louis CK. 2018. https://louisck.net/show/horace-and-pete [Accessed 22 February, 2018].

Manning, P. 2015. *Drugs and Popular Culture in the Age of New Media*. London: Routledge.

May, R., Remen, N., Young, D., and Berland, W. 1985. The Wounded Healer. *Saybrook Review*, Vol. 5, pp. 84–93.

McCabe, J. and Akass, K. 2007. *Quality TV: Contemporary American Television and Beyond*. London: I. B. Tauris.

Modeleski, T. 1991. *Feminism without Women: Culture and Criticism in a 'Post Feminist' Age*. London: Routledge.

Moreno, C. M. 2009. Body politics and spaces of drug addiction in Darren Aronofsky's Requiem for a Dream. *GeoJournal,* Vol 74, No. 3, pp. 219–226.

Nemeth, L. 2011. Nurse Jackie and Nurse Ethics: How TV and the Media Influence Our Public Image. *Beginnings, American Holistic Nurses Association*, Spring, pp. 8–10.

Nevins, J. 2018. Edie Falco: 'I've Never Loved the Work More, But I'm Not Cut Out for the Business'. *The Guardian*, April 11. www.theguardian.com/film/2018/apr/11/edie-falco-the-sopranos-outside-in-interview [Accessed 12 April, 2018].

New York AIDS Memorial. 2018. St. Vincent's Hospital: Why Is This Site Important to the Ongoing History of the Aids Crisis? https://web.archive.org/web/20131203013038/http://nycaidsmemorial.org/st-vincents-hospital [Accessed 12 March, 2018].

Nochimson, M. P. 2018. When Bad Things Happen to Good TV Shows: *Nurse Jackie*. January 26. http://cstonline.net/when-bad-things-happen-to-good-tv-shows-nurse-jackie-by-martha-p-nochimson/ [Accessed 1 February, 2018].

Ofcom. 2018. www.ofcom.org.uk [Accessed April 4, 2018].

Pajer, N. 2018. The 'Menendez Murders' Wigs Were More High Maintenance Than Its Stars. https://uk.news.yahoo.com/menendez-murders-wigs-high-maintenance-stars-151804584.html [Accessed 22 February, 2018].

Pearson, C. and Pope, K. 1981. *The Female Hero in American and British Literature*. New York: R. R. Bowker.

Phelan, P. 1993. *Unmarked: The Politics of Performance*. London: Routledge.

Pullen, C. 2012. *Gay Identity, New Storytelling and the Media*. Revised Edition. Basingstoke: Palgrave MacMillan.

Pullen, C. 2016a. *Straight Girls and Queer Guys: The Hetero Media Gaze in Film and Television*. Edinburgh: Edinburgh University Press.

Pullen, C. 2016b. *Pedro Zamora, Sexuality and AIDS Educations: The Autobiographical Self, Activism and the Real World*. New York: Cambria Press.

Quinones, S. 2016. *Dreamland: The True Tale of America's Opiate Epidemic*. New York: Bloomsbury Press.

Raphael, A. 2018. Edie Falco: 'I Started to Live My Life as Carmela!'. January 15, 2010. www.theguardian.com/tv-and-radio/2010/jan/15/edie-falco-nurse-jackie [Accessed 28 February, 2018].

Rasmussen, K. and Downey, S. D. 1989. Dialectical Disorientation in *Agnes of God*. *Western Journal of Speech Communication*, Vol. 53, Winter, pp. 66–84.

Ricci, F. 2014. *The Sopranos: Born Under a Bad Sign*. Toronto: University of Toronto Press.

Rinkin, S. 2000. *The AIDS Crisis and the Modern Self: Biographical Self-Construction in the Awareness of Finitude*. Dordrecht: Kluwer Academic Publishers.

Saad-Filho, A. and Johnson, D. eds. 2005. *Neoliberalism: A Critical Reader*. London: Pluto Press.

Sabibe, M. 2013. *Veiled Desires: Intimate Portrayals of Nuns in Post War Anglo-American Film*. New York: Fordham University Press.

Sanders, J. 2001. *Celluloid Skyline: New York and the Movies*. New York: Knopf.

Schlumpf, H. 2016. Nurse Jackie: Saint or Sinner? *National Catholic Reporter*, March 11–24.

Seiter, E., Borchers, H., Kreutzner, G. and Warth, E. M. 1989. 'Don't Treat Us Like We're So Stupid and Naïve': Towards an Ethnography of Soap Opera Viewers. In E. Seiter, H. Borchers, G. Kreutzner, and E. M. Warth (eds.) *Remote Control: Television, Audiences, and Cultural Power*. London: Routledge, pp. 223–247.

Shelby, C. L. 2016. *Addiction: A Philosophical Perspective*. Basingstoke: Palgrave MacMillan.

Skeggs, B. and Wood, H. 2012. *Reacting to Reality Television: Performance, Audience and Value*. London: Routledge.

Sloterdijk, P. 1989. *Thinker on Stage: Nietzsche's Materialism*, translated by Jamie Owen Daniel, Foreword by Jochen Schulte-Sasse. Minneapolis: University of Minnesota Press.

Smith, M. and Goodnough, A. 2015. Closing a Hospital and Fearing a Future. www.nytimes.com/2015/10/09/us/closing-a-hospital-and-fearing-for-the-future.html [Accessed 12 February, 2018].

Solstice. 2018. Solstice in Times Square. www.timessquarenyc.org/seasonal-events/solstice-in-times-square [Accessed 12 February, 2018].

The Truth about Nursing. 2018. History of the Truth about Nursing. January 22, 2011. www.truthaboutnursing.org/about_us/our_history.html [Accessed 12 February, 2018].

Tudor, A. 1974. *Image and Influence*. London: Allen and Unwin.

USF. 2018. Helen Miramontes: HIV/AIDS Nurse Pioneer, UCSF School of Nursing. https://nursing.ucsf.edu/news/helen-miramontes-hivaids-nurse-pioneer [Accessed 19 February, 2018].

Valliant, G. E. 1998. Natural History of Addiction and Pathways to Recovery. In A. W. Graham and T. K. Schultz (eds.) *Principles of Addiction Medicine*. Chevy Chase, MD: American Society of Addiction Medicine, pp. 295–308.

Warburton, N. 1992. *Philosophy: The Basics*. London: Routledge.

Weston, K. 1991. *Families We Choose: Lesbians, Gays, Kinship*. New York: Columbia University Press.

White, M. 2002. Television, Therapy and Social Subject. In J. Friedman (ed.) *Reality Squared: Televisual Discourses on the Real*. New Brunswick: Rutgers University Press, pp. 313–322.

Wlodarz, J. 2005. Maximum Insecurity: Genre Trouble and Closet Erotics in and Out of HBO's Oz. *Camera Obscura 58*, Vol. 20, No. 1, pp. 59–105.

Woods, T. 1999. *Beginning Postmodernism*. Manchester: Manchester University Press.

Yacowar, M. 2007. *The Sopranos on the Couch: The Ultimate Guide*. New York: Bloomsbury.

YouTube. 2018a. A Plea for Mercy: Law & Order True Crime: The Menendez Murders (Episode Highlight). https://youtu.be/zNCxFad6808 [Accessed March 7, 2018].

YouTube. 2018b. Law & Order: True Crime: Paley Center Panel: Edie Falco, Dick Wolf, Heather Gram. https://youtu.be/BTUG4W2w0x4 [Accessed March 7, 2018].

YouTube. 2018c. Edie Falco's Menendez Murders Wig Was Her Dream '90s Hair. https://youtu.be/OYl8g_s5h6I [Accessed March 12, 2018].

YouTube. 2018d. Anatomy of a Script with Nurse Jackie Creators Liz Brixius and Linda Wallen. https://youtu.be/l3-UP6l7l1c [Accessed March 12, 2018].

YouTube. 2018e. Clyde Phillips, Showrunner for 'Nurse Jackie'. www.youtube.com/watch?v=rwL3cnro-aU [Accessed March 12, 2018].

YouTube. 2018f. Nurse Jackie: Official Trailer. www.youtube.com/watch?v=5dpjMmSLjvQ [Accessed March 12, 2018].

YouTube. 2018g. Talk Stoop with Edie Falco: As Seen on New York NonStop. www.youtube.com/watch?v=LfusW8fx3x4 [Accessed March 12, 2018].

Zurcher, L. A. 1977. *The Mutable Self: A Self-Concept for Social Change*. London: Sage.

Nurse Jackie—Episode Index With Credits for Scriptwriters and Directors

Season 1

1. Pilot—Script. Liz Brixius, Linda Wallem and Evan Dunsky, Dir. Allen Coulter.
2. Sweet 'n All—Script. Liz Brixius and Linda Wallem, Dir. Craig Zisk.
3. Chicken Soup—Script. Mark Hudis, Dir. Craig Zisk.
4. School Nurse—Script. Christine Zander, Dir. Steve Buscemi.
5. Daffodil—Script. Taii K. Austin, Dir. Steve Buscemi.
6. Tiny Bubbles—Script. Rick Cleveland, Dir. Craig Zisk.
7. Steak Knife—Script. Nancy Fichman and Jennifer Hoppe, Dir. Steve Buscemi.
8. Pupil—Script. Liz Flahive, Dir. Steve Buscemi.
9. Nose Bleed—Script. John Hilary Shepherd, Dir. Paul Feig
10. Ring Finger—Script. Liz Brixius, Dir. Paul Feig
11. Pill-O-Matix—Script. Rick Cleveland, Dir. Scott Ellis.
12. Health Care and Cinema—Script. Liz Brixius and Linda Wallem, Dir. Scott Ellis.

Season 2

1. Comfort Food—Script. Liz Brixius and Linda Wallem, Dir. Paul Feig.
2. Twitter—Script. Mark Hudis, Dir. Paul Feig.
3. Candyland—Script. Rick Cleveland, Dir. Alan Taylor.
4. Apple Bong—Script. Christine Zander, Dir. Alan Taylor.
5. Caregiver—Script. Liz Brixius, Dir. Adam Bernstein.
6. Bleeding—Script. Nancy Fichman and Jennifer Hoppe, Dir. Adam Bernstein.
7. Silly String—Script. Liz Flahive, Dir. Paul Feig.
8. Monkey Bits—Script. Liz Brixius, Dir. Paul Feig.
9. P.O. Box—Script. Mark Hudis, Dir. Paul Feig.
10. Sleeping Dogs—Script. Liz Brixius, Dir. Paul Feig.

11. What the Day Brings—Script. Rick Cleveland, Dir. Paul Feig.
12. Years of Service—Script. Liz Brixius and Linda Wallem, Dir. Paul Feig.

Season 3

1. Game On—Script. Liz Brixius and Linda Wallem, Dir. Steve Buscemi.
2. Enough Rope—Script. Liz Brixius, Dir. Steve Buscemi.
3. Play Me—Script. Linda Wallem, Dir. Michael Lehmann.
4. Mitten—Script. Liz Flahive, Dir. Michael Lehmann.
5. Rat Falls—Script. Alison McDonald, Dir. Tristram Shapeero.
6. When the Saints Go—Script. Liz Brixius, Dir. Tristram Shapeero.
7. Orchids and Salami—Script. Ellen Fairey, Dir. Bob Balaban.
8. The Astonishing—Script. Rajif Joseph, Dir. Bob Balaban.
9. Have You Met Ms. Jones?—Script. Liz Brixius and Wyndham Lewis, Dir. Daisy von Scherler Mayer.
10. Fuck the Lemurs—Script. Liz Brixius, Dir. Daisy von Scherler Mayer.
11. Batting Practice—Script. Liz Flahive, Dir. Linda Wallem.
12. . . . Deaf Blind Tumor Pee-Test—Script. Liz Brixius, Dir. Linda Wallem.

Season 4

1. Kettle-Kettle-Black-Black—Script. Liz Brixius, Dir. Linda Wallem.
2. Disneyland Sucks—Script. Liz Brixius, Dir. Linda Wallem.
3. The Wall—Script. Liz Flahive, Dir. Seith Mann.
4. Slow Growing Monsters—Script. Ellen Fairey, Dir. Seith Mann.
5. One-Armed Jacks—Script. Rajif Joseph, Dir. Bob Balaban.
6. No-Kimono-Zone—Script. Liz Brixius, Dir. Bob Balaban.
7. Day of the Iguana—Script. Wyndham Lewis, Dir. Miguel Arteta.
8. Chaud & Froid—Script. Liz Flahive, Dir. Miguel Arteta.
9. Are Those Feathers?—Script. Liz Brixius and Liz Flahive, Dir. Randall Einhorn.
10. Handle Your Scandal—Liz Brixius, Dir. Randall Einhorn.

Season 5

1. Happy F**king Birthday—Script. Clyde Phillips, Dir. Randall Einhorn
2. Luck of the Drawing—Script. Tom Straw, Dir. John Cameron Mitchell.
3. Smile—Script. Liz Flahive, Dir. Randall Einhorn.
4. Lost Girls—Script. Michael Davidoff and Bill Rosenthal, Dir. Romeo Tirone.
5. Good Thing—Script. Cindy Caponera, Dir. Randall Einhorn

6. Walk of Shame—Script. Abe Sylvia, Dir. Seith Mann.
7. Teachable Moments—Script. Daniele Nathanson, Dir. Jesse Peretz.
8. Forget It—Script. Gina Gold and Aurorae Khoo, Dir. Randall Einhorn.
9. Heart—Script. Liz Flahive, Dir. Jesse Peretz.
10. Soul—Script. Abe Sylvia, Clyde Phillips and Tom Straw, Dir. Randall Einhorn

Season 6

1. Sink or Swim—Script. Clyde Phillips, Dir. Jesse Peretz.
2. Pillgrimage—Script. Tom Straw, Dir. Brendan Walsh.
3. Super Greens—Script. Liz Flahive, Dir. Jesse Peretz and Abe Sylvia.
4. Jungle Love—Script. Abe Sylvia, Dir. Adam Arkin.
5. Rag and Bone—Script. Ellen Fairey, Dir. Jesse Peretz.
6. Nancy Wood—Script. Carly Mensch, Dir. Keith Gordon.
7. Rat on a Cheeto—Script. Heidi Schreck, Dir. Jesse Peretz.
8. The Lady with the Lamp—Script. Abe Sylvia, Dir. Seith Mann.
9. Candyman—Script. Liz Flahive and Ellen Fairey, Dir. Jesse Peretz.
10. Sidecars and Spermicide—Script. Carly Mensch and Heidi Schreck, Dir. Seith Mann.
11. Sisterhood—Script. Liz Flahive, Dir. Brendan Walsh.
12. Flight—Script. Abe Sylvia, Clyde Phillips and Tom Straw, Dir. Jesse Peretz.

Season 7

1. Clean—Script. Tony Saltzman and Clyde Phillips, Dir. Brendan Walsh.
2. Deal—Script. Tom Straw, Dir. Julia Anne Robinson.
3. Godfathering—Script. Liz Flahive, Dir. Brendan Walsh.
4. Nice Ladies—Script. Abe Sylvia, Dir. Keith Gordon.
5. Coop Out—Script. Ellen Fairey, Dir. Brendan Walsh.
6. High Noon—Script. Carly Mensch, Dir. Adam Bernstein.
7. Are You with Me, Doctor Wu?—Script. Tom Straw, Dir. Brendan Walsh.
8. Managed Care—Script. Abe Sylvia, Dir. Jesse Peretz.
9. Serviam in Caritate—Script. Heidi Schreck, Dir. Brendan Walsh
10. Jackie and the Wolf—Script. Ellen Fairey and Carly Mensch, Dir. Jesse Peretz.
11. Vigilante Jones—Script. Liz Flahive, Dir. Brendan Walsh.
12. I Say a Little Prayer—Script. Liz Flahive, Clyde Phillips and Will Straw, Dir. Abe Sylvia.

Index

For Product Safety Concerns and Information please contact our EU
representative GPSR@taylorandfrancis.com Taylor & Francis Verlag GmbH,
Kaufingerstraße 24, 80331 München, Germany

Printed and bound by CPI Group (UK) Ltd, Croydon, CR0 4YY
11/04/2025
01843992-0006